BLOOD
AND
BROWN WATER

'I'm not a tourist...I live here.'

The other river war in South Vietnam.
Three tours on the brown rivers in I-Corps, the
Northern 'Brown Water Navy' boats.

Bob Johnston

For all of the 'River Rats' still
on their last run
somewhere on a shallow brown river
in a country so far from home.

Rest in Peace Brothers.
We, who survived to return to
the 'World', will work
to keep your memories alive.
That is our promise to you, we will
Never Forget
your ultimate sacrifice as long
as one of us remains alive

"Times"

It should have been the best of times,
it was the worst of times.
We should have been growing up slowly,
making boyish mistakes and living through them.
The mistakes we now made would cost a life,
if...that was all.
For many of us, without a doubt, this would be
our horrible welcome to manhood
and
our personal season in Hell.
Surviving it, evading Death's hand,
would change many of us forever.

Foreword

I have been living in Vietnam for 10 years now and I really enjoy reading about the various aspects of the Vietnamese / American war. The trouble with my mild addiction is that most of the books about the war seem to bleed together in my mind. They all show the horrors of war but usually from a front-line combat perspective. Whether it's from the foxhole or the cockpit the books are invariably the same in that they are about combat. This book truly comes at the conflict from a perspective that has not been explored. And to its credit it brings you directly into the conflict with personal accounts by a man that was there and aware. I love listening to an expert in any field. Reliving the river war through Bob Johnston's eyes and memories is to see and feel an expert at work. Blood and Brown water has its share of knuckle biting combat scenes but I loved the fact that it goes a bit more into the nuts and bolts of supply and the naval support that the troops, and especially the Marines depended on.

There are times when you forget the horrors of war. How messy and truly terrifying it can truly be. The stress that the tedium of waiting for the unexpected or expected action creates. Blood and Brown water reminds you of the terror and at the same time injects some humor into the mix. The in-country accounts of battles and rescues, attacks and defenses are spot on. I had trouble putting this one down for a bathroom break and dinner.

Foreword

These days I live very close to the River in Hoi an. Its not hard for me to imagine the strife and struggle that went on here. There are reminders if your eyes are open. The vine covered Bunkers and Pill boxes near the center of Hoi an. The small concrete bridge to Cua Dai that replaced the often burned and bombed wooden structure that was just a stones throw from the new bridge. But it's so peaceful now and it is an interesting counter point on how peace is better than war.

Seeing the whole picture from the supply side is enjoyable. I liked the scams and trades that bypassed the normal sanctioned delivery's.

So often we completely forget that the staples we enjoy need to be moved daily. Even in the middle of a bloody conflict. This book give you an insider's look at the vagaries and surprises that were an everyday occurrence to the men on the supply boats of central Vietnam. Bob builds tension leavened with action admirably. You will be enamored with his descriptive and knowledgeable point of view. A view that few have even known about, much less seen and lived through. Enjoy.

Philip R. Slocum
Hoi An, Vietnam 2016

Acknowledgements

I must give some thanks to a few people who pushed me back into, not only continuing to write, but also doing this book some justice following a rocky start with my first publisher. It wasn't easy after being gutted by them. Richard Botkin – 'Ride the Thunder', probably gave me the most encouragement to continue. Goose Gosswiller, fellow brown water sailor and writer, pushed, prodded and gave a wealth of information and timely assistance. It's due to his instance that I got back into the game, and, I would have never found Kim Birdsell and Kover to Kover. Kim is the editor/proofreader we all dream of finding but few actually do. Not only has she slaved over two of my books but also, the advice, notes and middle of the night email exchanges made things work.

I pay her, but – she has gone the extra mile to make the books take on a finished quality. Although separated by 13,000 miles and twelve hours, she's always there.

To all who buy the book, Thank you.

I knew when I sat down and typed the first word of the first chapter, that it wasn't about the money. It's about the unknown history of our unit. More specifically, it's about 'we few' – the 8-boat River Rats of NSA Da Nang (US Naval Support Activity) in the very beginning of the Vietnam War. We were few and we were scattered all over the I-Corps area of Vietnam. From the Arizona Territory, the South Chau Dai River, thirty some miles south of Da Nang, to the Cua Viet right up at the DMZ, we provided a constant supply of whatever the troops needed to continue and survive. Like them, there were no days off, no holidays and no excuses. We had a job to do and we did it any way we could...the best we could. This is some of the history of the first three years of the boat group.

Other books by the author:

Heart of War, Kindle 2016
Old Fool's Gold, Kindle 2016.

Table of Contents

`

Introduction 1

The stories written here are true for the most part, remembered the best I could after all these years. Although I did change some of the names, I didn't change all of them. I was given permission to use 'Frosty's' name and the pictures of him, by his family. Mostly everyone else is identified by either a nickname or a change in the last name of some kind.

The only reason I wanted to use not only Ken Brown's name but his picture is because he was (also) a wonderful guy. I may have the last picture taken of him and if I can get it to any of his family, I gladly will.

Most of the people written about in here were the best sailors in the world in one way or another. They were either brave or colorful beyond belief, wise mentors or wise asses, brilliant seamen/enginemen or outstanding NCOs. We, the 'River Rats' of the LCM-8's, were tasked with a job that could be boring, tedious or outright terrifying depending on the day and the river. Some days it was all three and more.

For a few years, on many rivers, I was associated with this wonderful bunch of guys. Since there is little or nothing written about who we were and what we did, not much 'official' history about us from the Navy, I decided to write a little myself, as well as some of the things I was caught up in. My feeling is that our group needs and deserves to be recognized; we should have at least a small spot in the history of this war. Our children, our grandchildren and a lot of other people should be told about and reminded of our challenges, sacrifices, how we lived and worked, relieved the endless pressure and died serving our country for that extra $65 a month.

Over the years, many of the memories of times and dates have gone, so I have tried to put it back together with some help. In many cases, I can sort of come up with the year when an event happened - the exact date is a problem and always will be. I can pin down a few dates; the deaths of some of the guys are a public record as is the date when the ramp at Cua Viet blew up or the Tet Offensive began in 1968. Those are easy.

I am typing this in June of 2004; it's been going on since about 1996. When I began the book I also began to fight with my own 'devils' of PTSD, so in some ways writing this is a sort of therapy. In other ways, its awaking thoughts that I have buried for years...decades, thoughts and memories that were better left buried, un-remembered and totally forgotten.

Some of the chapters almost wrote themselves, others took weeks or months. The one about Frosty and Ken took over a year to finish. My problem was writing a few lines and remembering the good times as opposed to their deaths that day. I would begin to cry like a baby at the stupid loss of them and have to stop. It remains the worst written chapter in the book and I can't change that no matter how much I try. In the end, I just finished it. It is my small tribute to the memory of two really great guys who died in their prime.

We were, for the most part, a merry band of brothers...sometimes a little too 'merry'.

Don Neff, who committed suicide rather than return for another tour, was a very good friend and companion. Alan Zaner was too. I haven't seen him since I left for Dong Ha in '66. I hope he is alive somewhere. The 'Mighty Quinn', 'Granny' Flagg, Lang, 'Fatman', Horace D. who taught me 'how' to be a boatswain's mate and, how to run an LCM-8. If I remember correctly, he was from Missouri, old bucket-mouth Horace D. was the best craft commander I served under. He was a teacher/mentor and all around great 'boss' and person.

The ironical 'Smitty', okay his last name was Smith. Other than that I only remember the picture in my head of him. Older gray, handlebar moustache, wise and in charge. When he arrived back in country in '68 it was a shock to see him. It was also nice to have him in charge of us in Cua Viet.

Black CPO Parrish, another good chief in charge of us up there. Found out from him that black guys could get sunburned and he had sunburn to die for!

Most of the rest I served with after 1967 are a blur to me. I was getting numb by that time and didn't form what you would call friendships. It was better that way, so when someone got killed you didn't feel the sense of loss; you worked together did the job and tried to stay alive. The rest of the time you tried to stay high or drunk. That helped a lot.

The (old) title of the book doesn't mean much unless you served in what became known as 'The Brown Water Navy' operating on the rivers in South Vietnam, the 'River Rats' as we called ourselves. I will explain this.

If you have ever been to a carnival, you know there was always a shooting gallery there. They called them many different things, but I remember one called 'The Duck Pond'(the original title of the book). There were about four rows of ducks with bulls eyes painted on them and big happy smiles. They bobbed up and down going straight ahead on their little row and the idea was to shoot as many as you could and win a prize.

That's the way we felt on the rivers; you were exposed and trapped with nowhere to hide, just like being in a shooting gallery. You were trapped into going in a straight line one way or the other. In 1968 we actually painted a bulls eye on my boat (on the bow) to give the enemy a target that was well removed from us.

Those painted-up ducks in the shooting gallery were inanimate objects anyway...no life, no feelings, no thought of fear. Us being alive was a different story, just like anyone fighting a war, we knew the white hot knife of fear. That explains the original title of the book.

I liked the original title – apparently, I was the only one who did and, it was a little too ambiguous to help sales. The more 'warlike' title seems to work better.

Our primary job was hauling much needed cargo, supplies and personnel up or down a river. Our secondary job was staying alive. Most of the time the 'bad guys' shot first and from a well-hidden position.

Most of this book is written a little tongue-in-cheek. Other than those times that you were scared out of your mind and trying to stay alive or drunk, you tried to have fun. Most of the fun was either doing something stupid or at someone else's expense. That's what kept us going most days and nights. I can look back on a lot (but not all) of the things that happened then and laugh about it now. I am saddened by thinking that although I survived, many didn't and I knew a lot of them.

If you are looking for a book of war stories I must apologize. Although there are a few of those in here, I've kept that stuff to a minimum. Most of the chapters leaning that way are more of the 'shot-at-and-missed' category and trust me, that has got to be the best feeling in the world when it happens!

I will also apologize for some of the language in advance. While I did clean some of it up, I also left in what I felt was 'enough' to convey the true spirit of the moment. Looking back I can probably count on one hand the times I heard someone use 'gee whiz', 'gosh-darn it' or 'shoot' as a colorful metaphor.

What I wrote about 'Frosty' Cain and Ken was tough. We were friends and how they died was stupid and pointless. The only good thing I can come up with about that incident is that we had just spent a wonderful day together and they both died instantly. We were all laughing when it happened. The pain of their loss seems magnified because, at that time, the Hue, Tan My area (at least for us) was pretty safe and secure.

The sub-title of the book was put on the camo cover of my pot (helmet) by me in the middle of 1967. By that time I figured I had enough time 'in country' (eighteen months) that I was no longer a 'tourist'. I was over halfway through my second tour of duty and either living on the boat or at the base camp, in a hooch or bunker, at Cua Viet (Camp Kistler), the river of the same name we hauled cargo on to Dong Ha/Quang Tri City on, 3.5 miles south of the DMZ.

Yeah, the DMZ, three and a half miles south of it. Our base was well within the range of the enemies Soviet made guns in the north. We were also pretty well 'benchmarked' by the local VC and other 'bad guys' in the area around us for the occasional rocket, mortar or 'other' surprise ordinance they wanted to use to just keep us on our toes…or dead.

Some other things about the book…

'It jumps around quite a bit…'

I agree, it does. There are a few reasons for this. The first one is that the I-Corps area has five rivers in it; they have back channels and tributaries. During my three tours, I was all over them. Not only that, but with new boats, new crews and new bases, I was bounced all over the damned place. Part of the reason is that I had boo-koo river experience and was (stupidly) good at my job. I realized that people depended on us. The Marines we hauled around and re-supplied, our NCO's back at the various bases and I tried to do my best to take care of my crews.

With just a few exceptions, the book is put together the same way that my tours were…patchwork…here today, there next week. There was also a lot of re-writing done. Most of what's in here is the truth, like I said above somewhere, remembered the best I could, through the fog of the years. All of this was lying dormant in my screwed-up brain. It began by writing a series of short stories then, assembling it into the book; that way you get a break between the very active chapters.

While I was writing the original book, I tried to find others I'd served with. I wanted some clarification and confirmation on some things I was about to publish. None of them, save a very small few, started to contact me until after the book was published – a few more popped up after I started to join some social media groups. Ya know what? These guys didn't want to add to or confirm things – they wanted to deny things I'd written about, shoot things down and correct 'mistakes' I'd made.

The problem is that, during the heat of action, under the duress of some circumstances, we all see things from a different angle. Most of what I am writing about here are things where I was directly involved in it – whatever it was – I was somewhere near or at the center of it...ground zero. I wasn't standing on the sidelines watching. I didn't show up after the dust had settled.

The Kindle formatting of the book is not perfect. This is a problem between Word and Kindle software – it took a while to figure this out. I did the best job that I could, without devoting my life to straightening it out. Trust me...I've seen a lot worse formatting jobs in some Kindle books – done by professionals.

Additionally – thanks to my first publisher – I stopped writing after a very bad experience with them; Publish America. They are pariahs.

I was urged back into it by some friends, wrote two more books then, after meeting Kim Birdsell (proofreader and editor) gave it to her for a good clean-up.

We had two unofficial mottos within the boat group.

The first one came up in something like 1966:
'You call, we haul, rain snow sleet or Viet Cong.'

This one (probably borrowed) was heard a lot after 1966-67:
'We've done so much for so long, with so little that now, we can do anything with nothing!'

With thirty-two months 'in country' on the 8-Boats on the rivers in I-Corps, South Vietnam, I believe I'm the only one that did that 'tour' for that amount of time on the 8-Boats for the NSA 'Somewhere' over there.

"What was it like...were you scared?" someone asks. It's very hard to explain to a normal person that most of the time was spent in sort of a numb state of being. You and your men were trapped into doing a job and under orders to do it. There was no way to refuse or get out of it.

You simply followed orders, did your job and tried like hell to stay alive and protect your guys. Before something happened, you always felt apprehensive and very on edge. When it did happen you were busy, very busy, and too busy to think or even be scared. When it was over, the adrenaline rush was still going on. Alive and in one piece, your crew safe and a whole boat still under you...that's when you get scared, real scared. That's when you begin to think about the next time and wonder if you'll be as lucky.

Very few of us were 'John Wayne'. That works real good in the movies, but in real life (when it's over) you almost destroy a cigarette getting it out of the pack then have a problem hitting it with the flame of the Zippo. Yeah, I can remember a few times when it was really that bad.

I felt betrayed by my government and my country following my time in Vietnam as most of us did. We were used, lied to and used as cannon fodder to further aims and ambitions beyond anything we understood...we followed orders and did our jobs.

I come from a military family and even though I felt no interest, I did pay attention to what happened in the years between. I never voted or allied myself with any political party or trusted any politician no matter how well he or she lied about what they would do to make our life better. I did however remain alert and aware of what was going on around me always. Some things don't change after you are subjected to something, like a few years in combat. It's hard to explain really. I watch what's going on around me and see things happening that other people around me seem to miss most of the time. Mostly small things that seem unimportant.

On the morning of 11th September 2001, I was on the road doing my job for the company that I worked for. I awoke in a motel room far away from home; got ready to take a shower and do the day's work, turned on the shower and the TV, then made coffee.

As a regular member of a few retired or other newsgroups, I was aware that there was a 'watch' on in the near east for some sort of terrorist activity. There had been a lot of things on the boards in the past year, lots of discussions on the 'way' it would be handled and all of the members (in most of the groups) suspected the worst.

I never made the shower.

As the small coffee pot burbled and burped in the room, the picture on MSNBC came to life. The camera was trained on Tower One. I watched as the talking heads wondered/speculated that it may be a small plane that had mistakenly flown into the tower, but how could this happen on such a sharp crystal-clear morning? I...realizing that I was never the sharpest pencil in the box also realized that (from the size of the impact hole) this was no 'small' plane that had hit the tower as they were speculating. Yes, it was a beautiful clear morning; even a blind pilot could see the tower. This was no accident but rather a pure terrorist attack...worse yet it was number two in the list of how it would be carried out. Number one on the list was a nuke in one of our ports, New York, San Francisco, Seattle - you pick it or all of them at the same time.

Turning to Fox News I found the same stupid questions being asked by each of the newscasters to the other. From what I saw in the damage to the tower, it had to either be a 737 or an Airbus if not a larger aircraft. The war of the terrorists was on and they (the newscasters) didn't have a clue.

How stupid were we? How little did they know? How hard was it to figure it out?

As I watched the pictures of the first tower burning and had the feeling that there would be many lives lost on that day, I caught the glimpse of the second plane flying past in a way that it could only be explained as 'aiming' at its target.

The airplane exploded through the second tower and I suddenly was just as pissed off as I was over thirty years ago. All of the feelings flooded back...I felt betrayed and violated and my country was being raped by something our government had screwed up, set up over the years proceeding this morning. We had been caught off guard. During the next hour all of my feelings came flooding back as I watched the TV. I became a patriot again after all of these years. For all of the innocents involved in this I wanted to kill...I wanted to get even!

Yes, it hurt me deep in my core to know that everyone on those jets...the two in New York, the one in Washington and the ones on Flight 93 were innocent American civilians. Businessmen going to work, wives and mothers doing the same thing or going on a trip, daughters and children going for a visit or to Disney World...

They would never reach the destination because of blind stupid hate.

Where could I sign up...?

Nowhere...I was just too old, no longer of any use to the Republic in a fight.

I felt too mad...too impotent...no longer able to help with anything that concerned saving lives. Frustrated, used, forgotten and totally abandoned. In a few moments I dearly wanted to serve again...again...get back in the fight for the first time in three decades...and kill.

Yes, kill some of the bastards that supported what had been perpetuated against the innocents here. Look one of them in the eye as I prepared to blow his brains out. I'm right you are wrong.

Any questions? Nope.

My views (after much research on the topic) have changed about what happened that day.

Introduction 2
In the beginning...

I joined the Navy in 1964; everything was full for boot camp in Great Lakes Naval Training Center, so I wound up in San Diego or 'Dago', as it was called by everyone in the Navy. Just like the song that was sung by the older recruit companies to the younger ones when we passed in formation on base, 'Mothball mothball don't be blue...our recruiter screwed us too.' Mine did. The new recruits were referred to as 'mothballs' because for the first week you smelled just like the mothballs our newly issued uniforms had been stored in.

Like the rest, I was promised everything. By the time I graduated from boot camp, not only were all the ships at full complement, but almost all the schools were full. I found myself stuck in one of the 'armpits' of the world (nothing worse than being a low rate in a Navy town) with not a lot to do and not much money to do anything with. During the next six months I went from mess-cooking to actually cooking to the security detail which was pretty good duty. Good, but boring most of the time.

I continued to apply to some schools that I had interest in, but never heard anything except that they too were full. I did have interest in sub school, but during the tank-test my poor sinuses blew that.

I had no money most of the time, Cinderella liberty, and began to think that I was in the service and trapped forever in 'Dago'.

Then one day a friend told me that they were looking for volunteers for duty overseas, in a place called Vietnam. We had heard some things about it, but not much. At that time monks were setting themselves ablaze in the streets and we knew that there were some advisors over there working with the country's troops. I mean how bad could it be, this was the Navy, we could pull some kind of duty on a ship over there right?

Wrong again...dead wrong!

Like a bunch of dumb kids we lined up and signed up then, as if we hadn't had enough fun up till now we were all taken to an area that was reserved for temporary housing for transient personnel and put in old barracks there. Now there was not only nothing to do, but we were at Coronado Naval Air Station and separated from everything by a canal or a sort of inlet. To go ashore we had to wait for the liberty boat! This was a liberty boat that ran a few times a day, mostly in either the morning or the evening, as more and more of us arrived the barracks became crowded and everyone was bored as hell. When the liberty boat arrived in the afternoon it was a mad rush to get the hell out of there!

No one had any idea of where we would be stationed or what was going on and the one thing that began to come to the surface was the mixing of rates (jobs); most of the rated personnel were SeaBee's. SeaBee's aren't shipboard rates but construction rates, shore duty rates, linemen, carpenters, heavy equipment operators, cooks, surveyors and the rest. As we got bored to tears, there was the feeling that we weren't going to be on any kind of ship. We were going ashore, but it was too late to un-volunteer!

After a few weeks we were not only overcrowded, but a real mix of rates and ages, everything from my group of un-rated guys straight out of boot camp to NCOs all the way to Chief Petty Officer. I should have suspected something, but was still young and naive; every single one of the petty officers had up to fifteen years of service and had been 'busted' multiple times. They had made rank then did something to lose it, more than once. The 'trigger' to what my outfit was about should have been one or more of them explaining to us young ones that they had been given a choice at a Captain's Mast, take a dishonorable discharge or volunteer for duty in Vietnam.

They didn't have enough time in to retire and had families so avoiding the old DD (dishonorable discharge) was incentive enough for someone to raise the hand and say yes. I mean hell Lang had six kids, or was that eight?

Although we didn't have to stand inspection there was the morning roll call, that was just to see who hadn't made it back from liberty the night before. It was pretty informal most of the time unless someone came up missing for a while, in those cases the shore patrol would find them and bring them back later. We sat for weeks on end, played cards or read most of the time and when you got really poor just went to movies on base.

It was August in 'Dago', the barracks weren't air-conditioned so, we melted in the humid stifling heat.

When the last guy arrived I clearly remember the head count 427, just like the Chevy motor. Finally one of the officers came around and there were meetings with the junior officers, the scuttlebutt spread that we were going to survival school of some kind. A few days later we were gathered together in our barracks groups and told that we were going to Camp Pendleton for survival school, what the hell was that?

By then there had been a loose chain of command or pecking order set up within each of the barracks groups, we had at least a junior grade officer in charge a higher ranking petty officer and a few below him. At least we were finally getting organized or as organized as we would get by then.

Survival school was sort of fun or at least it broke up the endless boredom of being stuck on base. Now instead of just heat and humidity we had that plus the choking red dust of Camp Pendleton as we marched, ran, drilled and got trained by the Marines. After a while it began to sink in that we weren't going to see a ship (as crew) during our deployment. Most of the Petty Officers in our group (especially the Boatswain's mates) had, at one time or another, been in the amphibious Navy.

It was pretty clear that we were going to be handling cargo or crewing landing craft, how bad could that be? I should have known how bad it could be or at least suspected something, we weren't being given intensive light and heavy weapons training for no reason at all! In the following years this training would come in real handy more than once.

While we waited the good old 'Canoe Club', as we cynically referred to the Navy, had other fun things for us to do. There were endless forms to fill out and the 'shot line' which was always exciting as hell, we got shots for everything but Rabies and the Clap! Thank God there were only about a thousand diseases in the world at that time…we got shot up and vaccinated for everything! There were days that some of us couldn't even move our arms!

My group was the last one to leave; we spent a week riding a C-130 from Miramar NAS to the airport in Da Nang, everyone else left on a jet! We hit almost every island in the Pacific that had a place to land, ate either boxed lunches or chow in the middle of the night on some island base in the ocean. They would radio ahead and tell them we were coming so they could wake up the cooks, while the aircraft was fueled and checked we ate whatever they fixed for us. We ran out of Right Guard a few days out and were really stinking by the time we finally made the landing.

My first view of Da Nang was through a small round window on the side of the C-130, we had left an Air Force base in Japan that morning, and it had been cold raining and miserable there; I had no idea what 'monsoon season' miserable was. It was now about sixty five degrees, in Da Nang, raining like hell and everything below was sort of a slate gray color covered with mist. I didn't know it just then but I would get used to this in the coming years...that and many other things.

9 November 1965, within a few days the first major battle of the war would begin in the Ia Drang Valley, things were heating up.

Update 2010

Since the original book was published a few things have changed in my life, some better, some worse, all interesting in their own way.

I'll make this kinda' brief.

As a nice part of PTSD, I had a dose of 'survivors' guilt'. I was also carrying around a ton of associated guilt from what we'd 'done to them' during the war. I hadn't thought a lot of what 'they' had done to us. What 'they' had done to their own countrymen. In 2005, I started making plans to return and thinking about staying there. With not much left as far as any kind of real family in the states, a few failed marriages and, watching what use to be my country, fall apart, there wasn't much left. When my mother died, that kinda' sealed the deal for me...I was gone as soon as I could put everything in order, in my life. Part of the trip was to say some final good buys, where the guys had died and lay some ghosts to rest – I hoped – finally.

I was going back to teach, hopefully change things for the better in the country and with my associated burden of guilt, atone for some sins.

In a few years and, learning more, this outlook and way of thinking would change. I'll explain that later.

Since writing the first edition of the book I've moved back to Vietnam. I taught ESL for 4+ years – until the school closed – then opened a little café in a backwater town on the south central coast.

Update 2010

By then I'd figured out that I was stayin' here. Tuy Hoa is about same, same 'Mayberry' and I call it that sometimes. In the past six years Bob's Café American has become well known, not just in the province but all over the world. Tourists – even the few we get here – tend to talk to others. We've also opened a little hostel called The Reef and are opening another café in Phong Nha, Ke Bang, close to where the main part of the plot in Old Fool's Gold takes place.

Welcome to Vietnam

It is interesting to note and to see how life can change in the span of a moment. And in fact, it often does.

When we lifted off the airfield in Japan that morning (the final leg of the trip) we had been listening to the steady (loud) roar of those four turboprops for about sixty hours, the same monotonous droning sound day and night. We were 'inching' our way across the Pacific Ocean. Late that afternoon one of the crew came back to us and screamed an announcement over the steady drone of the engines and he had to yell to be heard. I had a feeling, from the plane's changes in altitude and course, that we were (finally) almost there.

"We're about to begin our descent for Da Nang gentlemen...due to the possibility of enemy fire we will be coming in steep and 'hot'...thank you for flying with us and enjoy your stay in the garden spot of Southeast Asia."

Hey wait a minute...enemy fire and we're not even there yet? Yep this volunteering shit had gotten me in trouble again. I could blame it on Don Neff for talking me into it, but you can't blame something on a dead guy can you? I should have listened to my father when he'd told me to never volunteer for anything. That was good advice, not taken.

My father was a pilot; yours truly had a few miles in the air. Sure I trusted the guys up front because hell...they didn't want to be the first ones at the 'scene of the accident', but our flight turned into an amusement park ride almost as soon as whoever that was got back in the cockpit!

The plane did a sharp bank one way and we hung in our (netting) seats while it fell sideways. About the time we were level again we went down at a steep angle with power on while our stomachs introduced themselves to different parts of our bodies! The plane banked in the other direction, still making a power-on turn and we fell like a rock as the gear came down with the normal rumbling roar we were used to now.

As we leveled out again we were still 'sinking' (that means falling like a brick, but still sort of flying) pretty fast when the flaps came down and you felt that little 'lift' from them, at about the same time the nose came up and our stomachs tried to go you know where. We were nose up and still falling a little under full power, the turbines were screaming and the big four bladed props were making a lot of noise too but...things (sort of) settled out a little. I was looking at tops of trees going by outside of that little round window and wondering how the trip was really going to end when we hit the runway.

Yes, I said hit the runway. We hit with a thump that I'm sure put a real strain on the webbing of those seats, (how long is this runway anyway?). Power stays on then we get thrown against each other as the props work hard in reverse and at the same time someone up front is standing on the brakes and the 'cargo' becomes real close friends with each other! I guess the good thing about it was that it was over so fast no one had time to puke. Okay, you could call it landing, but it seemed like what my father would refer to as a 'controlled crash', thump bang screech!

Welcome to Vietnam...

Blood and Brown Water

I had no idea that this was just beginning three tours there; I had no idea that I would actually watch someone explode beside me, didn't realize that I would lose some friends that I would make in the near future. I would watch someone die that I could not help even a little bit and hold one of the best guys in the world in my arms while the last spark of life went out in him. Watch a loaded 8-Boat (Mike-8 or Mechanized Landing Craft) be blown up in the air over thirty feet, cringe in a bunker at night during an artillery barrage and wonder if we had enough sandbags on top of it.

Take a dump in a bucket because it was the only way to do it on the river, carry an M-2 carbine as a sidearm for a year, learn to love C-Rats (C-Rations or the standard field ration at the time) as a meal (packed in '45) because it was breakfast, lunch and dinner, learn to drink warm beer and like it. Save a P-38 that worked well and put it on the chain with your 'dog-tags' so that you didn't lose it. A P-38 is what we called the little folding can opener that was packed with the C-Ration meals. Not all of them were created equal, so when you found one that worked well, you kept it!

I could not even imagine that I would be the coxswain (boat driver) of a Mike-8 in hostile territory on the 'Duck Pond' for over two years, learn things that I didn't even want know about, hate a woman named Jane Fonda, learn to absolutely love Marines for the way they protected us on OPS (coastal operations on the rivers), just flinch a little as an 81MM mortar went off about fifty feet behind the boat one afternoon, get up in the morning and get ready to run the river again without a thought, have the clothes rot off of me during the monsoon season.

Take a bath (out of a bucket) in dirty brown water on a river, actually feel clean when I was done, never forget the high pitched whining sound that the engines air-starters made, the hammering vibration of the two big screws during hard cavitation, chasing down a destroyer off the coast to beg food then almost being left there when they got a fire mission. Going aboard an LST while it was being unloaded at the ramp and hitting the ships store for fresh cigarettes and candy, thinking about how good a cheeseburger would taste or almost anything that wasn't dehydrated or canned twenty odd years before.

Empty a full magazine into a sampan (a small Vietnamese boat) in '68...someone yelled 'grenade!' and all of us opened up. Four or five Marines and me...when it was over the young Vietnamese woman was floating in the water and the three guys in the boat were dead. Have White Phosphorus burns on my arm that finally went away a few years ago, check the uniform of a 'floater' in the river and if he was one of ours we brought him 'home', live through my last tour during Tet of '68 in Dong Ha.

For the most part I can still see, hear, feel and smell all of it, the smell of the brown rivers, ham and lima beans (one of the C-Rats meals), the odor when being downwind from a group of sampans in the river, heat-tabs to heat the meals (enough of these tablets were sent with each case of rations to heat the main part of the meal), the smell of death, the 'odor' and hissing sound that a small pill of C-4 (plastic explosive) gives off as it brings your water to a boil for morning (C-Ration instant) coffee, the smell of the smoke that hangs in the air after a firefight, and a lot more. The horrible sound that a 122MM rocket makes on the way in, to me it is still the most horrible sound in the world. If I close my eyes and simply think '122MM rocket' the sound comes back and my skin still crawls after over thirty years.

I still 'feel' the many other things now decades removed, but like a minute ago in my mind as I type this and remember more. The 'howl' of an incoming arty (artillery) round as it goes over, the unique sound of a Huey (UH-1B helicopter) or a bunch of them as they pass on their way somewhere, the stench of a bunker (you didn't go out to relieve yourself when it was raining steel), the melodic sound of an 8-boat's exhausts as all four go under water then 'burp' it out at idle, the admiration I had for my 'snipes' (enginemen) by pure luck I seemed to get the very best ones.

I will never forget the sound of a fifty caliber machine gun being charged with a round, a very positive 'ka-chunk' as the bolt puts the round in the breech. The steady hard explosions of them firing and the hollow 'clink' of the brass hitting the steel deck along with the belting, the smell of the hot gun oil as it burned off. It all still comes back crisp and clear after all this time.

How it felt to be 'short' (almost ready to go home) and worried that I wouldn't make it back to the 'world' (United States), the whine of those two big automatic transmissions as you put the boat in gear, the sorrow and the empty feeling I would have following the loss of two friends in the same moment, getting a boat back from Subic (re-fit and repair in the Philippines) and finding out that everything worked!

The joy of mail call that brought a letter from home or a 'care-package', a few of us being drunk as shit about half way through Tet of '68 discussing how we could make a self-inflicted foot wound get us out of there (and actually considering it), the very nice family that had the store off the ramp in Dong Ha they always had ice for the beer, pot so cheap that you rolled it big like a cigarette and so strong that it put you in a coma (almost), getting back in-country and finding out that my reputation had proceeded me once more, feeling so scared, so hopeless, depressed and angry that you just wanted to sit down and cry...then doing it once in a while. Six of us playing cards and drinking while eating one of my cakes from home with fingers and spoons, it had crumbled to dust in the month it took to get there, but we didn't care. Keeping an ARVN (Army of the Republic of Vietnam) platoon pinned down until they radioed for help. Okay, so why the hell did they fire at us?

Using 'ham and eggs' (frag hand grenades) to go fishing...well it worked, actually driving an M-60 tank off of the boat (that was neat), your hands shaking so bad that you couldn't light the damned cigarette, setting the 'head space' (the correct distance between the breach and the bolt) on a fifty cal. machine gun with a P-38 then finding out that it was right (you 'cranked' the barrel in until the P-38 was firmly 'pinched' then backed it off one click), finally finding a crew member that actually liked the ham and lima beans C-Rats meal!

How it felt to tell a captain just where he could stuff that Purple Heart and the look on the faces of him and his aid, a few days off because there was nothing to haul, tossing all of my ribbons in a 'shit-can' one day but vowing never to forget any of it.

Then trying to put it all out of my mind for decades.

The way the controls of the boat felt in my hand, kicking the 'wheel' with my foot then using my toes to make little corrections in our course. Playing 'Chicken' with another boat driver on the river and knowing when to flinch, pulling the engine stops at the end of the day and looking out over an empty, dirty well deck...finally. We had lived through another one, done our job and kept the Marines and Army guys up a river well re-supplied for another day.

Blood and Brown Water

Sitting on my chair in the con, on a sunny late afternoon after our last run, eating a dinner of cold C-Rats and semi-warm beer. Back loaded for our first trip of the morning and pushed up on the beach just a little sea-side of the ramp in Cua Viet.

Twenty years old, an E4 'boat driver', doing my job with the best damned 'Brown Water' sailors the good old USN had produced till that time. We few and so many others that depended on us to get the job done no matter what, the Brown Water Sailors of NSA, Danang.

In this book I refer to the enemy (Viet Cong) as we did then 'Charlie' and the more affectionate term 'Charles' or 'Chuck', we used other terms such as 'slopes', 'gooks' and 'gook-an-ese' to refer to all Vietnamese in general. These days I realize that they were people just like us...people not 'gooks', people.

There was total 'zero' glory or meaning in what we (the Americans) did, over 58,000 of us died in a very stupid war. We had learned nothing from history.

Making my first trip to the moving wall to say goodbye. then walking right up to the panel with two very important names on it (like I knew right where it was), touching them then crying like a baby. Taking the time to find the others I knew that were still on their last run on a river.

Realizing that my (second) wife didn't really give a damn, about anything that was messing me up, after all.

Finally reaching deep within myself and having the guts to contact 'Frosty's' family, then going further to actually visit them. If I could find Ken's I would do the same.

Welcome to Vietnam

Funny thing (sort of), I remember our NCO (non-commissioned officer) in charge finding me and telling me to beach the boat and get the hell off of it. My orders to return to the 'World', the land of the 'Big PX' had arrived, my replacement was on the way up from Da Nang and 'Smitty' didn't want me to get blown away while waiting for him to arrive at Cua Viet.

After almost three years in country, my rotation/separation/back-to-the-world date was in October or November of that year (by my figuring). Suddenly, in July 1968, I wasn't months 'short time' but days, hours, sooo 'short' I couldn't even see myself! Something had happened (and I still don't know what) causing the Navy to give me an 'early-out' of the war.

I was 'short' and stuck in Cua Viet, a few miles below the DMZ!

Suddenly I was more afraid than I had ever been so far...the fear is that you will die before you get out...seeing the light at the end of the tunnel and it is a train.

I gathered everything I owned and moved into one of the bunkers beside our hooch to wait for my replacement to arrive and catch a ride to Da Nang.

'Everything I owned' easily fit into a small Marine Corps field pack: there was probably my 'good' pair of flip-flops, one shirt (of some kind), an extra pair of shorts (cut-offs), shaving gear, soap and a toothbrush. A K-Bar, my wallet for my I.D, my orders, probably some things out of a few C-Rats accessory packs and the rest of my mags for the carbine.

That night we took about sixty rounds of mixed artillery fire in three to four hours.

I had my head buried in the sand in one corner of the bunker...God I didn't want to get killed now...I was so damned short! Survived all of this time to get blown away in the last day in country...no friggin' way GI! I hid in the bunker during the next day, only going out long and far enough to scrounge some C's, water and some beer.

That night we took about forty rounds of mixed ordinance over the same time span, seemed like all night to me.

I was still hiding out in that bunker when I was told that my replacement was on an LCU and would be there in a few hours.

The LCU had cargo going to Dong Ha so they didn't stop at our ramp at Cua Viet. They proceeded upriver with my replacement on board...in an ambush he was killed at about five miles upriver. An RPG attack took him and a few others out.

'Smitty' sent a runner to find me the next day and tell me that I had better get the hell out of there 'Di Di Mou' he said (leave fast, go away fast!). I was free to catch any ride I could find back to the Da Nang area.

This is what is strange as hell today as I type this:

I remember a 'Huey' sitting on the ramp.

I remember going over to it and asking for a ride and where they were headed for. They said, Da Nang...get my gear and jump on.

From that point I remember nothing until:

Being made to feel naked and useless by a couple of rear echelon non-coms in the processing area in Da Nang. Surrendering my helmet, my worn out flak jacket and most of all my carbine...I had lived and slept in the helmet and flak jacket for almost two years.

Welcome to Vietnam

My cut-down M-2 carbine had been at my side or within easy reach for the last eight months. I now had to clear and lock the weapon...snap out the taped-together thirty round magazines and surrender everything...

Even the rest of the mags in my field pack, all eight of them...

In my faded Hawaiian print shirt, my faded, rotting, cut-off Marine jungle pants and a pair of flip-flops, I now became a joke to them. Two guys that had no idea what it was like on the rivers or to be in almost daily combat but...probably wrote some really good 'war letters' home.

For the next few bone-clicking nervous as hell, scared out of my wits, feeling totally naked hours, reassuring myself that I wasn't going to die before boarding the plane...I would make it, I made myself as small as possible and waited. Officers gave me a look-over then avoided me. I was strange and very out of place. Holding my pack close, with my orders clutched firmly in one hand, I was just watching listening and waiting.

Then...

Walking across the airport in Da Nang for the last time to board a Braniff 707 for my trip back to the 'world' and carrying everything I owned in the world in a Marine Corps field pack. I didn't even have a Navy uniform. Cheering and clapping with everyone else when the wheels of that plane left the ground. The absolutely overwhelming feeling of relief knowing that I wasn't going back...ever. I had served my term and my country...over and out, as the Viets said in pigeon French/English 'Finny GI'...no more boom-boom, mama-san, cyclo-girl, noc-nam, sampan, booby traps, boats or monsoons...no more death.

Then...looking around the cabin and realizing that a lot of us were also...crying.

I didn't watch the news for a long time.

15 July 1968, at the stroke of midnight I'd turned 22 years old and didn't even realize that had happened. What I realized was that I was, finally, going home and never coming back. Or, that's what I thought then...

You Can Never Really Go Home...

You do go home, but in some ways you never do, in true absolute reality. Yes, there are some that have gone through combat and just put everything behind them, totally and completely left everything behind...forever. Some of us just have a way to do that and, return to being normal.

The majority of us were forever changed in some way or another. Some of us had that endless stare that we brought home and it never went away. Some seemed normal as hell until something happened one day and the big 'snap' happened.

A lot are like me. Seemed normal as hell for a number of years, your just average sort of screwed-up person that couldn't do much right but kept trying...and trying.

What you don't realize is way back somewhere behind you sits a sixty pound cement block. It is tethered to the back of your head by the world's biggest rubber band, all held by a little piece of rope and those rubber bands are kept stretched nice and tight for a very long time.

One day, when you least expect it, something happens and some idiot cuts that little rope. That's when your normal life ends. When that sixty pounds of concrete block hits you in the back of the head and holds reveille. 'Normal' is over.

If all you do is begin to cry once in a while, your family and all of your friends are pretty lucky.

You Can Never Really Go Home...

When my personal cement block hit me in the back of the head I began to cry and talk...no one understood. They still don't and they don't care to, nor understand. For a few years I became a little bitter over that, then, I realized that it was impossible for anyone to understand, let alone care. It hit me when I made my first trip to a moving wall to say goodbye to a few friends.

As I boarded that jet for my trip back to the 'world', I was unaware that on that day, my birthday, 15 July 1968, my entire life had been spared by what has to be the absolute irony. It had occurred just ten days earlier on a farm in Slate Lick, Pennsylvania, USA.

On the afternoon of 5 July (for unknown reasons), my family home caught fire and burned into the basement.

When I boarded that 707 in the early afternoon in Da Nang, I had no idea that literally, indeed, everything that I owned in the world, WAS in that field pack.

You can never, really, go 'home'.

It would be almost two full weeks until I found a family member to tell me I touch on this later, but here's what I mean by that. The thing is, if you've never been to war, never experienced it right in your face, you won't totally understand. If you have, then you know. War changes everything and everyone forever and that's a fact. Anyone who's been in combat knows the feeling. It stays with you, in you, for the rest of your life. The sights, the sounds, the smells, the feelings, all of it. You can close your eyes, think about it and it all comes back. Other things like sights and sounds, a piece of music, trigger thoughts and everything else. That part, in everyday life, is a real bitch to deal with.

For three years, I was cut off from 'normal' society. 'Normal' to me was Vietnam, normal was what you did every day on the river somewhere. My kind of normal was as far from life as you could get – the Vietnam normal I lived in for eleven months of the year was an alternate reality and I was used to that – it was my normal and that's where I lived and thought. The dose of real normal was a 360, back home, once a year. One day you're on a river – in thirty-six hours – you're home. That's not normal, no one told us what to expect, how to act, what to do.

You went from monsoon rains, being damp or wet most of the time, mostly cold showers and C-Rations – that 'you' cooked or ate cold – to a dry warm bed, a mother cooking meals, being fawned over and clean clothes – that weren't rags. Everyone being careful what they said or did because...they knew you were headed back in twenty-six days or less. Thirty-day leave ain't thirty days.

There is no 'decompression', things just change instantly. You're still in a reality that's far removed from what's real.

Your friends are all living different lives. Everyone you were buddies with are married, in college or have a job. They have real lives that you don't understand, you have a life that they can't comprehend – even if they try. In most cases you can't just 'hang-out' anymore...they have responsibilities, jobs, kids, families and bills to pay. In your reality the responsibilities are different...if you fuck-up someone could die and even when you don't, people still die.

You also can't just turn off the way you've lived for the past eleven months. Little things like, 'Would you pass the fuckin' potatoes please?' doesn't go over very well at the dinner table. Sure, there are laughs and giggles, but that doesn't mean it's accepted. It's tolerated. You shuck and jive at loud noises, you yell, scream and do strange things for no reason at all. You're always looking around, always seem worried about 'something'. You will sit alone and just stare into space once in a while, for no reason. You sometimes cry for the same reason...none.

You have your first beer before breakfast.

The second week your friends are all suddenly busy and can't hang with you anymore. They – some of them anyway – want war stories and you don't want to tell any. When you do begin to talk about some things, you also start to get real serious sometimes; they don't like that...

...what now seems like a lifetime ago, you had everything in common; now you have nothing n common – not even that beer in your hand...

...they also don't like it when you start talking about something, then for no reason that they can understand, start to cry and stop talking.

Something like the end of the second or third week, you begin to change. That's because you're thinking of going back. In too short a time this little episode of the 'Twilight Zone' is gonna' be over for you. You're thinking about that, in a week, in a few days, you'll be boarding a plane and headed back to what amounts to your version of reality – your 'real' reality. Once again, things will just flip back to the way it was.

Just as simple as changing the channel on the TV set...almost.

One day you're waking up in a nice warm dry comfortable and safe bed – a little over a day later you're laying down in a cot, in a hooch, along a river – if it's still there. You've been welcomed back and told that things are pretty quiet right now… 'we only took about twenty or thirty rounds last night…you can have your boat back in the morning, no fuckin' sweat – you got a new guy on the crew – be gentle with him at first, he don't know shit.'

You ask where so-and-so is, a fellow boat driver, 'He got hit last week, probably in Guam or Japan, in a hospital by now, wasn't too bad.'

He got a 'million dollar' wound; serious enough to get sent way back for care, but he'll live and he won't be back.

Yep, back to your reality…

.

NSA Da Nang and I-Corps

I have two letters of commendation in my service record. One was sent to our commanding officer by good old Billy Westmoreland for the outstanding job we did in Cua Viet. We deserved that one and we all knew it. We had done one hell of a job supplying our forces inland under some very bad conditions. We had managed to keep them re-supplied despite the weather conditions and almost constant enemy harassment. This was during the monsoon season, especially when nothing could fly we (the LST's LCU's YFU's and the Mike-8's) were the lifeline for the troops. We got the goods to a place so that truck convoys could finish the trip.

The other letter of commendation is pretty much a joke; nice to have, but sort of blown out of proportion. It's the one from our survey of the Dong Ha River in 66'. It makes us sound like lonely heroes on a valiant mission when in fact we just did a simple boring job and partied our butts off for about four months.

Charlie didn't waste any time or energy on us until he had a good reason to. Then he had a way of really making it count. That was during Tet of 1968 when the enemy made a very good attempt to close the operations on the Cua Viet River down.

NSA Da Nang and I-Corps

Our 921 boat after hitting a command detonated mine just up the river from the ramp at Cua Viet. Two KIA (out of a crew of three) and the boat/cargo a total loss. That's the bottom of the boat above the water; that is normally flat and not bent like a banana.

Pictrure: Bob Cross, NSA Danang

The YFU (Yard Freight Utility) 62 in almost the same spot as the 921. Another command detonated mine (one of our re-wired dud bombs from the DMZ). Most of the crew KIA or wounded.

Picture: Unknown photographer – public domain.

Beginning as the Naval Support Activity, Da Nang we grew with the stupid war over there and branched out to cover the I-Corps (Northern Province) of South Vietnam in about a year and a half. The overall unit was a mix of almost every rate (job) in the Navy.

We had buildings to repair and build, communications systems to construct, power and water lines to provide, cargo to move and people to feed. We also provided security. In 1964-65 there was a major build-up of troops in South Vietnam; my unit would become the backbone of their support.

In the next few years a lot of us would learn place names like: Chu Lai, 'Elephant Valley', 'Dodge City/Arizona Territory', Hoi An, Tan My, Hue, Dong Ha and Cua Viet. A place simply called 'The Bridge' would take on a special meaning for some of us and roughly a fifth of us would never make it back home to 'The World'.

While waiting for our equipment to arrive, we were housed at the old French barracks in Camp Tien Shaw across the river from the city of Da Nang. Being non-rated I was (along with a bunch of others) sent back to mess-cooking duties and I hated it. With a little bit of luck and a few months of waiting there was a call for boat crews. The cargo boats were arriving - LCM-6's and the LCM-8's. I got an extra stripe and became a seaman on an LCM-8. While more boats arrived we 'hot crewed' for a while, one boat and two crews to keep it running twenty-four hours a day, seven days a week.

There was no deep water pier, a place that the cargo ships could dock and unload directly on land. Our job was to run back and forth between ships anchored in the harbor and a sand ramp upriver past the city to unload. We ran day and night in all weather and did our job well. Most of our 'boat drivers' or coxswains had come from the Amphibious Navy. They ran the boats and taught their mostly inexperienced crews how to do our jobs with safety and pride. We got good at it. We also moved from the old French barracks to an LSD, anchored in the harbor during this time. My group was assigned to bunk in a troop carrying area in the bow, eight bunks high and six wide. In good weather the gentle swells entering the harbor rocked you to sleep. In bad weather you bounced in the bunk when a big swell went under the ship and the bow slammed down into the next one.

We were spoiled for a while, with good food, a nice ships store and hot showers.

The APL 5 tied up in Danang, early 1966. Picture Source: Public domain.

Within a few more months there were more of the LCM-8's and we went to single crews. At this time we moved to a newly arrived APL. The designation is Auxiliary Personnel Landing, a three story barracks barge left over from World War II. It was hard to figure out if we were going up or down in our living conditions. We did have hot showers, but the food was bad most of the time. We were at least tied up to a pier so unless the weather was very bad, it was comfortable. We could still go into town and there was now a big PX that we could hitch a truck ride to when we had time off. It was also around this time that the Deep Water Pier was finished at the mouth of the river. This had little effect on us as the harbor was filled with ships for us to unload day and night. At times we did our job so well (as did the crews loading us) that there would be a regular traffic jam at the sand ramp upriver.

Within a few short months, we became a hazy gray line of total and complete cargo, moving efficiency in Da Nang. Day and night our boats moved everything from beans to bullets ashore to keep the buildup going in the I-Corps area...our total effort won us our Naval Unit Commendation...from the Army Chief of Staff. Hell. We were just doing our job.

We were also feeling pretty safe and secure most of the time. The VC would hit the airbase Marble Mountain and a few places outside of Da Nang, but there was nothing like a real attack close to us. That was good because we didn't even have any weapons then. We just hauled cargo, massive amounts of it and kept the boats cleaned up and running. That was our job.

We had also been very relaxed until now and away from the stand inspection spit and polish 'real' Navy. Our first indication that this was going to change was a memo telling us that there was now a 'no wake' zone when passing the White Elephant while going upriver. I don't know where the name came from. The White Elephant was a big white official looking building that became the headquarters of NSA Da Nang. There was a dock installed right in front of it and one day a typical officer's motor launch was tied up there.

If any boat was caught making a wake in that area, we were told the craft commander would be 'written-up'. This was a form of discipline. Enough times and you could lose a stripe for it. Ok...now the 'chicken-shit' real Navy had landed. We were used to running the river wide open both ways. The next little memo hit us right where it hurt. We would begin to stand inspections, boat and crew, every Sunday morning. Promptly at ten AM, one of our boats would report to the dock at the White Elephant for this inspection. We were told that we would be in 'proper' uniform for the occasion and that it would be a real inspection. If the boat or crew failed it meant loss of liberty for the crew until you passed the next one...now that was the lowest damned blow of all!

To make it more exciting (for us) the inspections would be random. We quickly found out that, if we were lucky, the most notice we could expect before an inspection was about forty-eight hours. We were back in the real Navy of cleaning, chipping paint/rust, painting and polishing brass to keep our boats 'squared-away'.

The ones (of us) that had been in country for a while had nothing that looked like a real uniform. Most of us had totally converted to the Marine field combat uniform because they were easier to get, but more importantly, you didn't stand out. Our low cut Navy shoes had been replaced by combat boots and most of the time we only wore flip-flops (rubber shower sandals). There was a scramble to find someone about your size that had just joined the unit to borrow uniform bits and pieces from when the time came. Sort of 'I'll shine your shoes if I can borrow them for inspection' thing.

There was one other little problem here that everyone thought of right away. All of our boats were loaded with stuff we had sort of 'liberated' from the cargo we hauled. If the inspections were going to be real, that meant that some officer would be checking out the engine room and Lazarette or after steering area on the boats...damn...that's where we kept most of the beer! The only bright spot in this was that we would be given time off to go over to an area that was called Red Beach to clean and paint the boats. This was on the other side of the harbor and was pretty much a secluded area. We could work and party for a day.

We actually did a pretty good job for our first inspection. I was crewing for old Horace D. at the time and both crew and boat were about as squared-away as could be expected, given the circumstances. We had also put our beer, as well as other 'liberated' cargo, in one of the voids. These were hollow areas between the outer and inner hull. An 8-boat had seven of these and covered by a 'manhole' with something like sixteen bolts holding it in place. We painted the bolts and threads so that it wouldn't look like it had been touched.

We only got about halfway through our first inspection. BM-2 Lang saw to that in a very colorful way.

We had gotten all slicked up and took the boat to the appointed area. We tied up and old Horace D. presented the boat and crew for inspection in a snappy way to the officers and others present. We were to get off the boat and be inspected first so we got on the dock and stood at ease so they could look us over. One of the junior officers got on the boat and began his inspection in the con.

That's about the time we heard the Mike-8 coming upriver.

There was the normal nit-picking about our uniforms, shaves or haircuts, but nothing important. They always had to find something to bitch about or it wasn't a real inspection. The boat was getting closer and running wide open. The inspection crew was looking at it now and they didn't look happy at all; it was way past the point of beginning to slow down and not doing it. I seem to remember old Horace D. looking straight ahead and saying to me out of the corner of his mouth 'sounds like the 876.'

Due to age and other things, almost every 8-boat had its own particular sound. Most of it was the exhaust note, but some other things contributed and made each of them sound unique.

The four of us were all probably thinking the same thing, 'Slow down asshole!'

Nope...he wasn't slowing down a bit. The inspection party walked around behind us and gave us a chance to turn around and see who was about to catch a ration of shit. The boat was loaded very heavy and making a wake that had to be at least three feet high! The wake wasn't so much caused by the speed of the boat, but the flat ramp on the bow. Once an LCM-8 was fully loaded (and in our case most of the boats ran a little overloaded) that big ramp pushed a lot of water. It was about fifty feet from passing the dock; the officers had walked to stand on the edge of the dock right beside our boat as the 876 passed about twenty yards out in the river...wide open!

Those officers looked so cute in their nice pressed and starched white summer uniforms too, all that gold braid and fancy stuff, spit-shined shoes and all glowing in the morning sun.

Realizing where they were standing, Horace D. tried to get someone's attention, 'Sir...' they were more interested in getting the boat number and ignored him. Yep, it was 'Pappy' Lang. Worse than the wake was him shirtless and leaning over the con holding a can of beer up, yelling something that we couldn't hear over the noise of the exhaust and giving everyone on the dock the finger. He threw the empty can into the river and ducked down for another as he roared past us, throttles wide open and making his own little Tsunami. Ten AM and Lang was blown out of his socks! We saw the wake coming and before it hit the dock, we all backed up a few steps.

It was a floating dock, so when the wake hit it, it surged up and rocked at the same time our empty boat got slammed against it...hard! The reason we backed up and why Horace D. was trying to get the attention of the officers happened next. The water trapped between the boat and the dock had to go somewhere, so when the boat slammed against the dock, water shot up in the air about eight feet. All they needed was a bar of soap. While this was going on, the admiral's cute little launch was getting a slamming of its own a little further up the dock. Okay, it was funny as hell, but we couldn't even crack a little smile. Poor Lang was in a world of shit!

They had the boat number and left us standing there while they took off for the White Elephant. We held it until the three soaking wet officers were out of earshot (the one on our boat was dry), then just broke up laughing. We also figured the inspection was over. With them occupied on something else we untied the boat and left to get changed into our 'regular' uniforms...back to work.

Although we did find out that most officers are not 'boat smart', we also found out that none of them saw the beer can. Lang took a bust down to second class petty officer and finished his tour a few months later. That alone was probably worth giving the officers a good 'bath' that morning.

Forth Trip of the Day...Cua Viet River, '68

At just twenty-one years of age. I was a veteran of combat duty in South Vietnam, the craft commander of an LCM-8, a fast river cargo boat that weighed over fifty tons empty. I was responsible for the boat, but more importantly, the three crewmembers under my command. We had to function as a unit. This was my third crew and my fourth boat since being made a 'craft commander'.

I had learned my job well. I can make a Mike-8 'walk and talk', I can read a river, see the sandbars and the current...find the channel...remember the many rivers and the quirks they have. I have learned to look, but most importantly, 'see' what is going around us to (maybe) keep me and my crew alive and safe.

Ramp scene at Dong Ha 1967, three 8 boats and a YFU. The center 8 boat has a cradle in its well deck with a 10,000 gallon fuel bladder. Public domain.

At twenty-one years old, I am a 'vet' and an 'old-timer' to this 'Cherry' first tour crew. I am totally full of life and committed to staying alive. I am brash and bold. I have survived firefights on the rivers, mortar and artillery attacks, RPG's and mines. I feel invincible sometimes and seem bulletproof to them, my new crew. Still scared sometimes, I feel the same way, but somehow more cautious...when nothing is happening and it's cool.

Hell, I was 'in-country' when Da Nang still had 'liberty'. This meant that when you weren't working (on duty) you had free run of the town. It had been shut down for over two years and on ops you didn't go anywhere. If you were going more than a hundred feet from the boat you had your M-14 and a few extra mags of ammo, you wore your pot and your flak vest most of the time...the times they were 'a changin'.

Leaving any ramp or anywhere that you were beached, you did it in style. The taxpayers owned the boat, but you didn't even think about that. You were the craft commander with a loaded boat and on the way...or...unloaded and going for another load somewhere up or down a brown river. You are in charge of the throttles and the helm and have four supercharged GMC 6-71 diesels at your command. You leave any place by gripping both of the Morse engine control handles and pull back all the way. The engines growl as both banks go into reverse and the two thirty-six inch propellers bite the water.

The two automatic transmissions make their usual low whine and the thick black smoke pours from the water level exhaust ports. You have idled the four big diesels for nearly an hour and it's time to clear their throats and put the spurs to the boat. Run hard and fast again, run fast and stay alive for another day.

As the boat backs down you do a fast scan of the gauges on the instrument panel in front of you. The tachometers jump over to 2000 RPM then settle back down to around 800; everything else is normal. The engine temps are good and the air pressure is coming back up to 175 pounds. You also look around as you back the boat off the ramp. Quickly you scan behind you and around you because you don't want to back the boat into another that may be around and trying to hit the ramp as you leave.

Almost fifteen-hundred horsepower makes the boat vibrate as you back off the ramp in reverse, then find neutral and coast for a few seconds...just a few seconds. You coast back clearing a few other boats that are either being loaded or unloaded...on a ramp, on a brown river.

You move the ramp control into the up position then, watch as the big air-powered rams lift five tons of steel again.

The other boat crews around you watch as you back down. There are waves, smiles and 'gestures' as your guys do the same in return. There was a very tight camaderie on the boats.

As the huge air rams pull the ramp up, you spin the helm with your foot and ease the controls into forward, pushing on the two control handles to ease the engines into 'all ahead fantastic'. Escaping air puffs and hisses as all of the controls are worked to get the boat back on its run, the other crewmen (un-rated seamen) walk to the bow on the narrow gunwales on either side of the well deck. He spends the trip scanning the water ahead of the boat for floating mines.

The 'all ahead fantastic' is a joke. The Mike-8 has a top speed of 13.5 knots, which is about eight miles an hour. Your 'snipe' or engineman has disconnected the governors from the engines...your speed can be about 16 knots or a blazing ten miles an hour! Still about eight miles an hour loaded, somehow you feel like you are a little safer and flying.

There are only two types of boats that can outrun you on the rivers (where we were then), the PBR's (light patrol boats that are our security) and the new and bigger YFU Skilak landing craft.

Our PBR near the mouth of the Cua Viet River. Public Domain.

The boat shakes like hell as the screws bite water again, pushing it behind you and forcing the boat to get under way. It comes around to the way the rudders are set, hard over and leaving wherever you are under full power. You never 'baby' one of those boats.

You straighten things up, look out and find the channel...the place you came in from about an hour ago, coming downriver. As the boat comes up to full speed and the engines settle into their uniform roar there is another quick scan of the gauges by you and your 'snipe'. He taps one that isn't reading right, making it jump and settle in like the other three. You exchange smiles before he steps out of the con.

After lighting a cigarette you pick up the radio handset and call in:

'Base niner one three (your boat number)...under way for Dong Ha.' Release the button and wait. The response from the ops bunker takes a few seconds:

'Roger niner one three...permission to run the river.'

You respond: 'Niner one three out.' Then lay it back in the radio pack.

There is no one around you...no other boats...you are making the last run of the day to Dong Ha. There is just enough daylight to get there, get unloaded and get back to Cua Viet for the night. You watch the banks of the river and keep your heads down a little as you don your 'pots' and flak jackets once more. There are no Vietnamese anywhere on the banks to be seen. You are on your own and at full throttle. After a few minutes you call base and ask for permission to test fire the 50's and other weapons, permission is given and your 'snipe' gets behind the guns to make sure they still work.

Getting behind the mount he charges the guns, yells 'Clear!', swings it over to the bank and unloads about twenty rounds. As he looks at you and smiles (the mount is working), all hell breaks loose from the riverbank! He woke up some NVA that were dug in; in the next few seconds my snipe and gunner unloads everything towards the area that the tracers are coming from...and the B-40's (rocket propelled grenades or RPG's).

The B-40's? You could knock them down with a broom if you had one. They seem to come at you slowly, but are deadly on impact. This time they miss and explode in the water far on the other side of the boat.

It was brief, intense and shocking, but now behind you. The fire has ceased, you have run past it, but mark the spot to watch on the return trip.

This time, unlike some other 'gunfights' on the river, we fired first, but at nothing. Normally they begin with good old 'Chuck' opening fire from an ambush position (bunker) on the river bank and scaring the hell out of us.

Your 'snipe' just unloaded about one-thousand rounds of 'mixed' fifty caliber directly at the area that the fire was coming from and 'Charles' stopped. There is a cloud of dust hanging in the still late afternoon air in the area from the pounding it took in less time than it took to write this, your ears are still ringing from the muzzle blast. You now do two things that are very important as more ammunition is brought to the mount; light a 1945 vintage Chesterfield from the C-Rats four-pack with shaking hands and then call the location in to the base. The Marines on patrol on the north bank of the river, may want to look the area over for a 'body count' in the next few days. If my snipe got lucky.

Geez guys, we didn't mean anything, we were just checking the weapons!

Laws of Combat

With my apologies to Murphy and a few others...

When in doubt...keep firing

2. If it's a spare part you REALLY need, it's not available.

3. When in doubt...duck

4. Most days happiness is defined as a full automatic, belt fed, large caliber weapon

5. Don't worry about the round 'with your name on it' – worry about the one addressed to 'occupant'

6. The simple things are almost always impossible

7. The radio works until you REALLY need it

8. The pin is always harder to put back 'in' the grenade

9. Don't volunteer until you're ordered to

10. If it's stupid and works, it ain't stupid

11. If there is a better plan, an officer didn't come up with it

12. Everything you need to survive was made by the lowest bidder

13. Beer- 'A beverage made to be stolen and consumed, even warm'

14. Anything you do can get you shot at, this includes doing nothing

Laws Of Combat

15. Some C-Rations were never meant to be eaten

16. If the 'other guys' look really friendly, chances are they aren't

17. If the enemy is in range, so are you

18. Try to look unimportant...they may shoot at someone else

19. A lot of things made to operate in combat probably won't

20. The 'last' round probably isn't...wait and see

21. Never stand near an officer, they may miss and hit you

22. Tracers really do work, both ways

23. Never stand when you can sit, sit when you can lay down, stay awake when you can sleep, pass up hot chow or a cold beer

24. Experience is something you get, right after you need it most

25. The deepest part of the river is where the enemy put the mines

26. That new kid playing with the tear gas grenade will pull the pin...then drop it

27. Junior officers are just like you, but with all the common sense removed

28. Don't ever be the first or the last

29. No combat-ready unit has ever passed inspection

30. Visa-versa applies to the above

31. When a junior officer comes up with a plan, just do the opposite

32. Combat always happens at the worst possible time...the same applies to 'Dear John' letters

33. There is always enough room for more ammo

34. If you can't get it through normal channels, steal it .

35. If you are 'sneaking' somewhere, the enemy already knows you're coming

36. The new boat will always break down first

37. It's a bad idea to run out of cover, river and ammo at the same time

38. The spare part you waited two weeks for will be the wrong one

39. The last round in the red-hot fifty will cook off

40. If you needed something yesterday, you'll get it next month

41. Mines are equal opportunity weapons

42. Bunkers were made to be slept in

43. If one layer of sandbags is good, three are better

44. Anything you can put between you and the enemy is better than nothing

45. The first round in one of the guns will be a dud

46. When you really need air or artillery support, they are busy somewhere else

47. A five second grenade fuse will only burn for three seconds

48. The most dangerous thing in a combat zone is an officer with a map

49. If two things are required to make something work, they are never shipped together

50. There is always a way

51. A sucking chest wound is your body's way of telling you to slow down

52. When a plan sounds really good...it probably needs more work

53. Let someone else stick their head up first, the bad guys may still be watching

54. Never lead when you can follow, that way someone else gets chewed out

55. 'Experience' is the worst thing to have most of the time

56. Military intelligence is an oxymoron

57. Every order that can be misunderstood will be...at the worst possible time

58. A moving target is harder to hit...move faster

59. Never draw fire...it irritates everyone around you

60. When you need an officer in a hurry, take a nap

61. The cavalry never comes to the rescue

62. If you lose contact with the enemy, look behind you

63. Killing for peace is like whoring for virginity

64. When you've secured an area, don't forget to tell the enemy

65. Never worry about 'three guys on a match', it's that one idiot with the Zippo

66. If you can't remember, the Claymores are pointed at you

67. All-weather air support doesn't work during the monsoon season

68. Remember #1 and fall back on it as needed

Camp Tien Shaw

Camp Tien Shaw was across the river from the main city of Da Nang South Vietnam. It was an old French compound that nothing had been done with for years before we arrived. Our advance SeaBee units had started to rebuild it about six months before my unit began to arrive in-country, most of the barracks buildings were pretty bare and some didn't even have electricity or lights. There was a chow hall and an EM club set up, a central sort of bathroom and showers, but that was about it by then, November 1965.

Our C-130 taxied to what had been a terminal at the Da Nang airport, unloaded us and our gear so that we could mill around in the drizzle, try to find a place to hide from it and wait for the trucks to take us over to the camp, our home away from home.

Since we had been forgotten, we all just stood around for a while or sat on our sea bags and relaxed. We got nice and wet waiting for our transportation to arrive. Our introduction to Vietnam was wet and very humid; the other thing that was pretty overpowering was the smell. There was an odor like a garbage dump that sort of hung in the air all of the time. This was the background 'smell' of any city in Vietnam. You got used to it after a while. The other thing we had coming was the culture shock of our first truck ride over to Camp Tien Shaw.

We were dumped in a completely foreign world to say the least.

Nothing had prepared us for the sights or smells of this place we now found ourselves in, the dirt mud filth and squalor of a true third-world country in the middle of a war that would drag on for many more years.

When the trucks finally arrived we loaded our gear and our wet butts on for the long, slow ride to our new home. It was slow because the roads were narrow, muddy and filled with pot holes that were worse than spring in Pennsylvania. Some were huge. The road was also very well choked with traffic - military and civilian.

On the way to Camp Tien Sha, we got a short tour of the place we would come to call 'Dog Patch'. This was a collection of hovels, houses, workshops stores, bars and brothels that we would get to know well in our off-duty time; a true slum.

Processing us didn't take long once we unloaded in the camp. A few clerks took our names down on a roster, then sent us to a building where we could draw the supplies we needed. You were given a folding cot, a blanket a mosquito net and then issued one set of Marine 'greens', combat boots, mosquito repellant and a field cap before being assigned to a barracks building.

There was no indoctrination, a pep talk or anything the first day. We simply found the building and dumped our gear, set up the cot and the netting.

These buildings had been built by the French in the early 1950's. The walls and floor were concrete and the roofing was corrugated metal. The trick of moving in was to find a high dry spot on the floor...the roof (in most of the buildings) leaked when it rained and it was still raining. I was also lucky enough to get assigned to one of the ones with no power (yet). We had Coleman lanterns.

We spent the first evening hooking up with some of the guys we knew and getting to find out what was going on...not much at all.

The boats hadn't started to arrive yet, but there were other things to do. Most of the non-rated guys were either assigned to some kind of clean-up detail or sent mess-cooking. The best news was that after evening chow was over the (make shift), Enlisted Men's club was open. Although the beer was mostly flat and warm...it was beer!

There were showers when the water was turned on, sometimes there was even hot water. My first trip to the 'head' (showers/bathroom) was something that I'll remember forever. If you are reading this and you were in one of the first groups to inhabit Camp Tien Sha, you'll remember it too.

The toilets didn't work and if, by chance, you found one that did work, it stopped working the next day!

It seemed that there was so much work to do that our SeaBees hadn't had time to work on the old French toilets or the plumbing under them. The old 'water-closet' fixtures didn't work and the drains were plugged or broken. Few things were worse than hunting for one that wasn't totally full (to use), then trying to hold your breath long enough to use it! At least the showers worked.

Every morning began the same way for at least my first week or two. Get a quick shave and shower before the water was turned off, hit the chow hall for breakfast while dodging the trucks and helos 'fogging' to kill mosquito's, then show up for morning 'muster' and see if they had something for you to do. If not we could break up the boredom by hitching a ride into either 'Dog Patch' or all the way to Da Nang, have a few beers then make it back for evening chow call.

So many of us had been dumped there in such a short period of time that even the paper-pushers were way behind in handing out even the most 'crappy' duty. Broke, bored and tired of doing nothing (which can be hard at times!) I grabbed mess-cooking duty before something like cleaning the toilets came along or something even worse.

My 'even worse' was about six months in the future.

The one thing I made sure to do was stay in touch with anyone that would maybe be assigned to a boat crew. I kept on good terms with the guys (Boatswain's Mates) like Flagg, Lang and old Horace D., so when more boats showed up I was ready to get out of that chow hall and I made sure they knew it!

Sometime after Christmas in '65, an LSD (landing ship dock) or two puked a load of boats in the harbor. Suddenly crews were being called for and made up. I managed to get assigned to one of the freshly delivered Mike-8's in a hurry. I knew little about seamanship or the boat I would be assigned to but I thought I could pick it up as I went along...I was right. My one buddy Don Neff and I were assigned to the same boat a few days later. I went on as a seaman and Don went on working under the 'Snipe' as an apprentice.

Each boat had two crews then, the shifts were twelve hours on and twelve off. Relief (crew change) happened mostly by a ferry boat, you packed aboard then went for a ride looking for the boats that the crews belonged to. Depending on where your boat was this relief could take up to an hour.

There were no radios in the beginning; your particular boat could be in the harbor being loaded, going up or down the river, at one of the small piers or the sand ramp. You found out by asking other crews where they'd seen your boat last.

In many cases you found them on the river, you went alongside long enough to jump off while they jumped on the relief boat. As both boats got back underway, the crews shouted things back and forth about where they were being loaded and the condition of the boat. If we missed the 'where' part of that, you just went looking for a load in the harbor; there was enough to go around for all. Pick a ship, go alongside and hope someone spoke at least a little English.

Check the cooler to make sure the previous crew had stocked it with ice, beer and Cokes. We had the old style galvanized Igloo water coolers and almost any of the ships would give us more ice. In the harbor or running the Da Nang River we were in a nice breeze away from the stink of the city, the humidity and heat.

What is an LCM-8?

Until about 1975 it was probably the best steel hulled, flat-bottomed, medium sized landing craft the US Navy ever had.

It was designed and built during the Korean War as an expendable landing craft with one purpose - deliver an M-48/60 tank and its support equipment to the beach. Nothing fancy and it was delivered as a one-trip boat. Considering how well they were designed, I really found this hard to believe, but during a war I guess, everything including people is expendable. The job just needs to get done.

During three tours on the rivers in Vietnam, I found out just how great this boat was. At right around 100,000 pounds of solid steel it was rock solid in the water, empty it only drew four feet of water so it could operate in a deep creek. Flat bottomed and without a keel it still only drew about five feet of water with its full 100,000 pound cargo load (or more) on some days on the river.

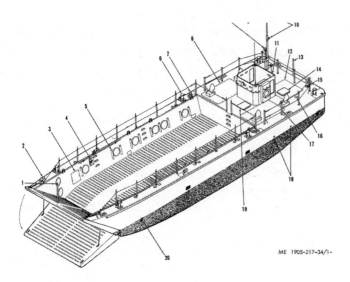

ME 1905-217-34/1-

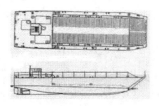

The recessed 'well-deck' of the boat was almost fifty feet long and twenty feet wide. The bow ramp could either be let down easy or done in a 'free-fall' way when in a hurry. Done this way, the solid steel five-ton ramp would hit the ground with one hell of a thump in about a second. Normally there were two large air rams to move it up and down. What made this boat truly amazing was its agility in the water...and half way out of it. Whoever designed this landing craft had a true gift. Seventy-four feet long and twenty-four feet wide, hitting the scale at fifty tons empty, it was a dream of a medium landing craft. What made it so good was hidden under the main deck.

Blood and Brown Water

I spent a few years and thousands of miles on various rivers standing on top of four GMC 6-71 diesels, supercharged no less. These four engines were arranged in 'banks' of two, each pair drove a large automatic transmission. Behind the shafts were two thirty-six inch tugboat screws (props) that had amazing power to move water and anything else in the way.

When the boat was empty you could bring it to a stop (from full speed) in about two boat lengths and you could turn it around in its own length. Once you learned how, you could 'walk' the boat sideways. Not bow/stern/bow/stern, but a straight sideways walk like parallel parking on the water, but easier than in a car. You could do it on the run or stop and walk it in then tie up. If you needed to make an adjustment on the way in or out you simply used the throttles to speed up or slow down one of the banks and change the attitude of the boat.

The two things that I found amazing (when I was taught how to run a Mike-8) were just how easy it was to move the boat in shallow water or have over half of the boat out of the water (dry) and still be able to get free.

Those two huge screws and the flat bottom were a very good combination, as long as they had water to move the boat driver could use it to his advantage. I have been in water so shallow that the bottom of the boat was bumping along the river bottom as I backed us out. All I had to do was bring the RPM up a little and force more water under the boat as it lifted on the swell and moved back, ease up on the throttles and allow it to settle. Repeating the act could move the boat back half a length at a time, even with about thirty tons in the well deck.

And, once taught how to do it, hitting the beach was very easy in everything but high surf and windy conditions, even with a full load. You learned the boat, learned how to read the surf and 'ride' it in. With a little practice and paying attention a fully loaded beach landing could be made with just a little bump.

What it was built for – an M 48/M 60 tank in thewell deck. There is still enough room for a truck, a Jeep and a few pallets of general supplies.

When putting a newly arrived boat in service we did a few things to make them livable, sort of adding 'creature comfort' to a place that you would be spending a long work day on. Later, on coastal ops, the boat became your 'home' and doing these things (as well as some other additions) became even more important for crew comfort. With most boats, the first things you did was scavenge enough wood to build a canopy over the 'con' (wheelhouse-control) area and put a raised wooden floor in the con. Some of the other things that followed as time and material allowed were seats for the boat driver and sometimes the engineman, a sort of table in the area behind the con to store things, on prepare food, etc. These things were done while the boat was put into service hauling cargo; there was no time off given for construction.

With massive amounts of supplies to move ashore in Da Nang and only a small pier to accommodate ocean-going ships our boats worked twenty-four hours a day, seven days a week. We became an endless haze-gray floating supply line. The boats were serviced, repaired, fixed and painted on the run.

Blood and Brown Water

One day on the Cua Viet River, I had a howitzer in the well deck and they wanted to find out if we could put them in a stable position to fire and then move. On the Cua Viet, we had a tidal effect that could raise or lower the river a few feet, depending on the time of day. Our group NCO was Chief Parrish then and he had great confidence in my boat handling. He went along on the trip and was touting me and the boat all the way upriver. It was nearing late afternoon as I pushed up on shore the first time and the crew of the howitzer began doing some 'benchmarking' from that location.

We moved two more times and on the last one had an extended fire mission. I had beached the boat very hard to give them a good solid platform to fire from. As the extended fire mission went on, the tide was going out and the river was going down. Parrish continued to tell them that there was no problem as I got more and more nervous; the gun crew enjoyed throwing rounds into the DMZ as my boat was becoming higher and dryer by the minute.

I did not want to spend the night three miles up the river with no security.

Finally, Parrish walked back to me and asked what kind of shape we were in. I think I remember telling him that we had to move the boat or we were in some serious shit. Almost sixty percent of the boat was high and dry, but I had been checking and there was a still lot of water under the stern. We had about fifty tons of mobile gun in the well deck...but...it was well forward, we were not straight on the river bank but at about a forty degree angle facing upriver.

Having learned my job well, I fired the engines up and allowed them to warm up a little. If I blew one up, the 'snipe' standing beside me would kill me! After a few minutes of letting everyone sweat a little, I put the helm hard left and pushed the engine controls slow ahead…then more…then more until the boat was shaking a little and beginning to move with the stern going upriver. Not much, but a little.

I was slowly pivoting on the flat and deepest part of the boats bottom as I attempted to swing the stern to the right. I got about ten feet of movement, but not much more. Moving the engine controls into reverse I allowed the two big screws to suck up some river water and push it under the boat. It almost moved then so I let them sit there for a while in reverse and wash away sand and mud from under us, not fast so there wasn't a lot of vibration from cavitating screws, just enough.

The other important thing I had learned was to move the rudders from full one side to the other, which washed a 'hole' under the stern of the boat. We sat there as I made a hole under the boat and it just 'wiggled' a little in reverse. We were still high and dry on the river bank.

Once the 'hole' was washed out, my real ace-in-the-hole was that fifty tons in my well deck…all the way forward. I had Parrish ask them to fire it up and back all the way to the rear of the well deck. As they did I backed down very hard. They moved the weight aft and our stern went down about two feet as all of the weight was taken off of the deepest part of our bottom. Parrish smiled at me as we backed off the river bank and into the river…mission accomplished.

Hue August 5, 1967, the Death of 'Frosty' Cain and Ken Brown

I know there were many others that went through a lot worse than this, for a fact I know of a few companies of US Marines that lost more guys in a minute during an ambush. They lost a lot of guys simply protecting their supply line and the 'River Rats' that kept that supply line moving...us.

I guess the reason that I will always carry this memory with me is two-fold, Forrest 'Frosty' Cain was a good decent upstanding person as was Ken Brown and they both died in a senseless way in a very stupid war. I guess the thing that hurts the most is that we were in a pretty safe area at the time, coming back from a very nice day on the town in Hue.

This has also been the hardest chapter to write.

It has proven to be very short on words, but long in time to finish, I have tried so many times to sit down at the keyboard, suck my guts up and just put the words down so it's done...for the last time. The last time didn't come until I had a few shots of 'Jack', a few beers to wash them down, that same old catch in the breath and the lump in the throat then the tears, a grown man crying and typing away.

This jumps around a little bit and I will apologize if it's hard to follow. I have tried (as I said above) to just get it done. This is just the way it came out.

Hue August 5, 1967, the Death of 'Frosty' Cain and Ken Brown

Yes, I have been to the wall and I have touched the names of the dead. I have gently stroked my outstretched fingers over all of the names of those that I knew, over that cold hard granite surface that can give remembrance, but not life. I have remembered too much about the ones that I knew all too well and then stood there and cried like a baby.

I carried home a few rubbings of the names.

I shared the same birthday with Forrest 'Frosty' Cain.

I met his family for the first time a few years ago and we spent several days sharing memories. You see, they never really knew how their son died or lived over there.

This is an unusual picture of Forrest 'Frosty' Cain. First – he's standing still, not working on something and, he's squinting, not smiling as he always did. He was one great guy just to be around.

Blood and Brown Water

BM 2 Ken Brown, a fellow 'boat driver' and all around great guy. He left behind a wife and (as I remember) two young children.

I spent the last few moments of the lives of Ken Brown and 'Frosty' Cain with them, on a canal bank between Hue and Tan My. It was a beautiful day, sort of cooler than most. We had a borrowed Jeep and were singing something stupid while going down the road back to the base. '99 Bottles of Beer on the Wall.' We had a lot of fun that day and were just on our way back to relax a little more, pick up the work in the morning and do our job as always.

A single round from a lucky sniper ended our fun in an instant.

In the records this 'incident' is recorded as a 'jeep accident'. In reality, a single round from a sniper's rifle killed 'Frosty', who was riding 'shotgun'. He apparently slumped against Ken who lost control and we went over the side of the road, rolling down the bank into the canal.

I clearly remember the jeep suddenly veering out of control, then rolling down the canal bank. I see it in slow motion. I remember dust, then water, then the jeep on its side.

The three of us in the rear got our wits about us after it was over and pulled both of them free. We dragged them back up close to the road and tried to find wounds, revive them and see what we could do to save them. Nothing…they died in our arms.

I remember screaming at 'Frosty', ripping his shirt open to find the wound, yelling at him not to die but hang on, slapping him hard and then…'Don't you die…don't you dare die on me!' We had both guys up on the bank of the canal…they were dead and we were peeking over the top of the bank cautiously looking for the where the sniper was. Other than our two 45's and a few mags of ammo, we were unarmed.

(Appropriate profanity at that moment excluded). They were both dead, nothing we could do would bring them back now. A single bullet had killed them both. Ken died of a broken neck when the Jeep rolled over.

As the (now) senior person, I don't remember being scared at the time, but I do remember realizing that it had to be a sniper. I'd not heard anything. 'Frosty' was the only one hit and there had been no other fire. We were miles from our base, in what had suddenly become hostile territory, two dead buddies and a wrecked jeep. If the sniper was still out there and we stuck our heads up someone else was going to get 'popped' by him. We had no pots or flak jackets. Our only option was to stay down and hope that someone came along to help out. We gathered weapons, ammo mags and watched. One of the guys checked the other side of the canal for movement. I peeked over the top of the bank once in a while, also watching for anyone approaching through the rice paddy. It was quiet and still except for a few water buffalo moving around.

We were 100% defensive. With only those two 45's and three mags of ammo each, two dead buddies, no body armor or 'wheels', we were trapped. At least until it got dark.

After probably half an hour we heard the familiar sound of an approaching six by six. It was a Marine patrol moving down the road toward Hue at a leisurely pace; trucks and jeeps. We saw each other at about the same time. They rolled to a stop putting a screen of vehicles between us and the opposite side of the road.

I talked to the sergeant in charge of the patrol explaining what had happened. Once stopped, his guys were 'on point'. Once everyone realized that it had been a sniper, every tree, building and mound within range came under close scrutiny by the platoon. While they helped us load Ken and 'Frosty' into a truck, anything that moved out there got hit with heavy machine gun fire and hit hard!

They turned around and took us back to base.

I remember a short debriefing by the chief petty officer and our officer in charge. Near the end of it, one of the corpsmen came in to verify how they had died. That's about the time I went numb. I did help get some of 'Frosty's' gear together, but in the end I wound up in our little club simply getting totally shit faced drunk.

The three of us were put on the 'inactive' list for a few days; I don't remember much of those three days. I do remember the grief that settled over me in an alcoholic haze - that and an overwhelming feeling of total rage.

I was transferred to Cua Viet a few weeks later.

Hue August 5, 1967, the Death of 'Frosty' Cain and Ken Brown

Frosty's portable welder coming back from a repair visit to the Marines, across from Tan My. They loved him because he was always over there repairing/welding a 'Track' or another vehicle.

On my second trip to Tan My I had met them both. Ken Brown was a fellow boat driver and 'Frosty' Cain was in charge of the boat repair shack, actually 'Frosty' was everything to everyone at that time. He was the total embodiment of a Navy Sea Bee, 'Frosty' Cain could weld, build, weld more and keep a boat running. He even helped the Marines out by going across to their small base and welding up wounded Amtrak's tanks trucks and anything else they needed fixed so it could go back to work.

'Frosty' was not only a hard worker and the class clown, but also one of the best 'comshaw' artists in the Navy, if you needed it he could find it. He had the true gift of finding something that you and your crew needed, then delivering it. He always had a smile, he was always looking around and we could always get good 'hootch' from him. If your boat was broke he would jump in and help your 'snipe' get it fixed. He did everything with a little humor and hard work, one of those guys that could make something like chow-call an occasion. Once I met his family I understood/realized why 'Frosty' was the way he was.

Ken Brown was on the other end of this. He was a very nice and decent person, he was sort of quiet and reserved in a way. Ken was an all-around nice guy.

After that I stopped being close to anyone over there, no more friends. I didn't want to really know anyone else that was probably going to die as well as them.

One Very Dumb Incident

This is one pretty good example of just how stupid things could be at times and, as you will see it wasn't our fault. We were only helping a friend...seriously!

On what was probably the third trip upriver for the day, we were back loaded with C-Rats and pallets of 155 rounds for the ramp at Dong Ha. It was late fall in '67 and things were pretty quiet on the ole' Cua Viet River; they had been for a while and we were relaxing a little as we moved cargo. And boy were we moving cargo, the eight LCM-8's stationed there (by then) were making at least six trips a day to Dong Ha and back. The one boat was a designated 'bladder-boat', with a big rubber fuel bladder (in a wooden cradle) filling their well deck. They did nothing but haul fuel all day. The rest of us moved pallets of cargo, ammunition and vehicles. What no one knew was that our buddy 'Charles' was taking a break before trying to kick the hell out of us again, but he would wait until just before Tet to do it.

Before we left the ramp at Cua Viet that day, a platoon of Marines approached the boat and bummed a ride with us. This was not an unusual thing and we did appreciate having the extra firepower with us always, just in case.

The platoon moved aboard and took up positions in the well deck around the cargo as the back loading finished and we prepared to get underway. I liked the fact that I saw not only the usual M-60 heavy machine gun, but more than a few LAWs (light anti-tank weapons), a few guys carrying M-79 grenade launchers and a 'rocket' (bazooka) guy.

I talked to the platoon leader and we had a smoke while loading finished. We were about the same age and had about the same amount of time in country. My offer of cold beer was declined and we were out of pot so we couldn't help them too much.

The Pettibone forklift operator stacked the last pallet on and I raised the ramp in preparation to leave. After calling in to get clearance to run the river I backed off the beach and moved into the channel for our run upriver calling in "Eight seven six...under way."What came back over the radio was the standard reply from the local smart ass on duty in the comm (communications) bunker "Roger dodger eight seven six...over and under...have a good trip, over under and out."

At 'all ahead fantastic' we began our next to last run of the day. There was a little wind from the South China Sea, but as we came up to running speed, everything became calm around us, dead calm. No wind and no noise, except the engines under us running very hard, putting out a steady deep throaty exhaust roar.

It was a beautiful day with hardly a cloud in the sky and, for a change, the temp was down as well as the horrible humidity. Even with no wind it was comfortable on the river. About the time we were kicking out of Cua Viet I heard Bucci calling in that he was leaving Dong Ha. He had been running the bladder (fuel) boat for a few weeks and we would be passing in about half an hour, him empty me full.

It was very relaxed on my boat. There was no pressure and there hadn't been any action for weeks. We relaxed and the platoon did too. They are going into combat and thinking about a lot of things, mostly just staying alive and making the end of the tour.

Just about where I figured it would happen, I saw Bucci's boat coming downriver. We are going to pass in an area where you can see for miles in all directions, the riverbanks are only about five feet high and the fields are only Elephant grass and some corn on both sides. There are a few tree lines, but they were well back from the river, probably close to a hundred yards. As we were about to pass (the boats were around thirty yards apart) I saw a bunch of splashes in the water between his boat and the river bank. The platoon leader saw the splashes at the same time. We were both looking at the tree line about then and clearly saw muzzle flashes and a little smoke. I don't remember being scared, but being suddenly really pissed-off!

As another group of splashes appeared in the water close to his boat, Bucci and his crew were looking in the direction of the tree line too. In a flurry of activity, my snipe was on the fifty and the platoon leader got his men up. Some of them were looking in that direction and had started getting weapons ready even before anything was said. As the boats passed and we had a clear field of fire, the command was given and everyone opened up on the tree line. I put the boat in neutral, a few of the Marines climbed up on pallets, my snipe opened up with the fifty and walked the bursts into the tree line. Their guy with the M-60 opened up and all of the riflemen began firing.

The only reason that I can think of to explain why I would even think about putting the boat in neutral while we were under fire could possibly be stupidity! I remember doing it and maybe thinking we were somehow protecting the other boat while they got out of the area? Probably not. It was more a case of we had more firepower and were a little pissed-off just then.

I mean our perfectly beautiful day had just been completely ruined!

I do remember, with absolute clarity, standing in the con watching the splashes in the water and wondering when the first rounds would begin hitting us.

As the boat slowed down, everyone was on target and there was a cloud of dust rising from the area of the tree line. Our tracers (from the heavy machine guns) were bouncing into the air in all directions around that area.They were being pounded, the splashes (in the water) stopped suddenly. While I didn't hear anything on 'my' radio, the radioman with the platoon had been on his calling it in, at about the same time that we saw both white and green smoke grenades popped at the tree line the radioman yelled at the platoon leader to cease fire.

It seems there was an ARVN (Army of the Republic of Vietnam – the ones on our side!) unit along the river that was taking heavy fire from 'a boat'. They were pinned down and requesting assistance! Before the platoon leader took the handset from his radioman, we exchanged a look that was one of those 'what the hell?' ones. Maps came out, followed by a quick exchange on the radio to verify the position of the unit and our position on the river (hell we knew the answer anyway) yep it was an ARVN unit.

His conversation continued for a while as I got the boat back under way for Dong Ha and everyone relaxed a little. After something like that you are pumped for a while so you don't really relax completely. I questioned myself about calling it in, but decided against it. I'd probably be hearing from our NCOIC at the base shortly anyway. Why start a conversation when you don't have all the facts?

For the remainder of the trip we sort of huddled-up and made sure that the one main fact was straight...yes...those morons in the tree line had fired first!

I was right. As we beached at Dong Ha there was a Marine officer standing there waiting for us and he had a strange smile on his face. I gave my snipe the boat and got off with the Marines. As we approached the officer he just shook his head, but was still sort of smiling. He asked us "Okay...why did you assholes fire on an ARVN unit? And by the way, you (meaning me) call your base."

We explained what had happened and a few of the other Marines backed up our story. We had all seen the rounds hitting the water near the other boat andwe had also clearly seen muzzle flashes and smoke from that tree line. They had fired on us or at least at Buccis' boat. Why would a friendly unit just fire at us when they knew we were on their side? No one knew. We were the only boats on the river; 'Charlie' did not have boats up there hauling cargo.

I got back on the boat and got our NCOIC (non-commissioned officer in charge) on the radio. With his usual 'proper' radio manner he asked, "What the fuck did you do, John?" Bucci wasn't back yet and his radio wasn't working. I explained what happened. After listening to my side of the story he said, "Okay, look don't fire on any more friendlies...at least not today...I'll try to find out what the hell happened."

Bucci did confirm that there had been fire from that area (at least he thought so) and there were 'dings' near the bow of his boat. He had taken a few hits from small arms. We never found out why an

ARVN unit had opened fire on the boats that were obviously 'friendly', but we did find out that they had taken no casualties, which was good.

First Trip to Dong Ha

I was actually given a choice about going on Coastal Ops by our groups' chief. It was sort of an offer I couldn't refuse…I figured it beat the hell out of being busted back to seaman and going to the brig. After all I had just made E3 a few months before.

One of the slang words you learn early on in the Navy is 'comshaw', which means steal, but in a nice way. We didn't steal things that belonged to other personnel; this was reserved for 'liberating' things that you needed mostly, but not actual theft. If you needed parts or supplies that you couldn't get through normal channels or would take too long (which it always did) you just 'comshawed' them.

An example of how upside down the supply system was could be illustrated by being able to go to the PX outside of Da Nang and buy all the Kotex you needed, truckloads of it and you just went in and bought it. On the other hand, if you needed a new screw for your boat, even though you could see them piled in the supply yard, you had to put in a written request and wait…forever! The only way you got something like that in a hurry was if the screw actually fell off.

Anyway, doing a little 'comshawing' opened the door for coastal ops.

The harbor and river in Da Nang was a very busy place. As more boats arrived we went to twelve hour shifts and were really hauling cargo. We got at least Sundays off once in a while and that was usually a time for going to Red Beach and painting the boat, but we could also party there. The rest of the time we were either under way somewhere or tied up to a ship in the harbor getting loaded.

The good news was that since we hauled everything and the crews loading us didn't always take too much care handling the cargo, there were always broken pallets. We usually didn't have to break into anything it fell out.

Most of the boats had stockpiles of stuff stashed all over the place, lots of canned food, some fresh food, cookies, candy and almost anything else that was on its way to shore. Most importantly we hauled beer and we seemed to haul a lot of it! The strange thing was that a lot of these pallets were damaged in some way...funny how that works. We were never greedy or obnoxious about it though. We only took a few cases out of each pallet and some for the other boats. At one time I remember us having at least a hundred mixed cases stashed in one of the voids. That's a lot of beer for one boat. Okay, we didn't want to run out. We always had ice too because we could beg it from the ship we were being loaded by.

None of the security people ever questioned the damaged pallet; there were no real manifests for our loads and no one ever checked the boats, at least until a green craft commander screwed up on one trip.

That would be me.

We were hauling beer that day, but we had a lot on the boat, at least enough for a few days. Just about the time we were ready to hit the sand ramp upriver in Da Nang, someone discovered that we had a pallet of Olympia staring us right in the face! Out of all the beer in the world - Olympia! Most of us were used to this very good beer from being in California and this made grabbing some of it impossible to resist. I mean we had to have some priorities...didn't we?

Now the sand ramp was normally pretty busy in the afternoon and a lot of times we would have to wait for someone else to leave so there was a spot clear to beach at, but not today. There were some open spots and we could pull right in. As I remember, I handed the boat off to the snipe and had one of the deck hands jump down in the engine room. I cut into the back of the pallet and started passing the cases of beer down to him while the forklift began to unload us. There were just two little problems involved here.

There was a sentry actually doing his job for a change.

The beer was on its way to the officer's club...which was the worst of the two.

Nothing happened until the next afternoon when we were being offloaded at the deep water piers which, by the way, had just been opened. It was a boiling hot day and we were all fighting for shade and sweating out butts off when the CPO of our boat group showed up and wanted to talk to me...in private.

He was very nice about it. We had always been on good terms and got along very well so he was trying to save my ass in the only way possible. Calmly and quietly he explained that I was in some pretty serious shit. He had talked to the CO about it and explained that I was a good boat driver and overall a good sailor. It helped that I had also been a volunteer for duty here. If...I went along with what they had decided, I wouldn't go to Captains Mast (and probably get busted just after making E4). I could volunteer for coastal ops and leave in the next few days...which I agreed to in a split second.

There was only one little hook thrown in...he had also assured the CO that I would sign up for another tour. I figured what the hell, how bad could it be...I bent over.

Looking back through the haze of time and experience, the things I would go through in the next two years, a little brig time and a bust would have been a better choice. A mere walk in the park...on a sunny day.

Dong Ha and the Cua Viet River

In July of 1966 there were two boats sent from Da Nang north to the Cua Viet River just south of the DMZ for the purpose of seeing if the river was navigatable from the mouth of the river to the bridge at Dong Ha City. At that time the only personnel at the mouth of the river were a company of Marines protecting civilian contractors; our other objective was to haul cargo upriver to the ramp at Dong Ha. There was a ramp being built at the mouth of the river by these contractors that would eventually be used as a staging area for cargo to be transported upriver to supply Marines operating in the area. We thought we were going for a few weeks, but I wound up being there for about two months that time. We had no idea how big this would get.

Following my little brush with military law, I got a new crew, but got to keep the 913. We were teamed with another boat driven by a quartermaster named Quint; he had been the only other person from our group to be on a river outside of the Da Nang. He had taken a survey crew somewhere and returned about a month before so he had 'experience' and it was thought he could lead us to and navigate the Cua Viet River. Get us there, read the river, find the channel and be sure we could get to Dong Ha loaded with cargo.

I was about to get a crash course in coastal navigation and learn how to read a river the hard way, one sand bar at a time. In the near future these things would come in real handy for me and my crews.

As we prepared to leave, we were told not to talk to anyone about this super secret mission. It was like the fate of the world hung on us and our two boats. I mean our commanding officers made us feel like James Bond. We weren't allowed to leave the APL; they issued us weapons and our orders. We were hooking up with a convoy of LCU's going to Hue the next night; it was timed so that we could break-off at daylight and continue to the Cua Viet getting there at mid-morning. Our destination was some sort of base camp at the mouth of the river. Everything was very hush-hush and we took it seriously (for a while).

Oh...the weapons? Everyone was issued an M1...yes...this was 1966 and we were carrying frigging M1's. Oh My God! That and two bandoliers of ammunition, twenty 'strip-clips' each, even I knew that if we ran into 'Charles' we should just surrender. Quint and I were each issued a 45 as a sidearm and three mags of ammo. Wow I really felt safe then!

We hung out on our boats and became heroes to everyone else. Wow we were going into enemy territory, sort of like the Enterprise going where no one in the boat group had gone before...we even had guns and shit, that was impressive! I think it was the next night that we 'secretly' hooked up with the U-Boats to head north. They were fully loaded for Hue. We were very lightly loaded with supplies for the base camp and a few pallets of beer...right, beer. And if anyone touched any of it I was gonna shoot them!

We had to follow those slow assed LCU's for most of the night, which was a pain! But you have to imagine how good we felt, apprehensive and a little of that scared/excited feeling, but we were getting away from what was becoming the 'real' Navy in Da Nang. There would be no more inspections to put up with and, from what we'd been told, there was just a job to do for a while up there. No one knew how long, report to the Marine CO and go to work, survey the river to find the channel then just keep running back and forth to Dong Ha.

There was no idea of what we would run into as far as the enemy being active in that area. We did know that we would be living and working just a few miles south of the DMZ, right under Uncle Ho's nose.

As we went seaside and began to ride the gentle swells of the South China Sea, made a few miles then turned north for our destination we were relaxed and content. Everyone had a beer open and we were listening to Hanoi Hanna on the little radio (hell she played the good tunes). She also had a news flash that night "For the United States Navy LCM-8's 860, the876 and their brave Navy sailors...enjoy your trip boys, you will soon die in Vietnam. Your families will be saddened and grieve over your senseless loss in a country where you have no business fighting." Okay, she got one boat number wrong. I'm sort of glad that the rest of the message was wrong as well.

Okay...so much for the James Bond shit.

That proves that one law of Murphy's (or someone's) if you are sneaking somewhere the enemy already knows you are coming.

That night was also the first time I really got the shit scared out of me! We had been running up the coast for a few hours (slowly because the U-Boats we were following were loaded and really slow) most of us were relaxed and getting bored. They were going so slow that I had shut one bank of engines down and I was just idling the other one. I was just at the helm watching the lights of

Quint's boat to keep my distance right and wishing the trip was over, some of my guys had sacked out on the cold deck.

All of a sudden there was an explosion of noise on both sides of my boat, a thunderous roar! Seconds before loading my skivvies I realized that they were a couple of what were called 'Nasty Class' boats (like a PT boat)...ours, at least the ARVN Navy. They had radar, we didn't. The U-Boats had radar and probably not only knew that they were back there, but had talked to them on the radio (which we also didn't have).

Those assholes probably enjoyed exploding out of the pitch black night behind us and scaring the shit out of a couple of blind boats. Okay, we were all awake now.

Sometime after dawn, the U-Boats turned and headed for the entrance of the Perfume River on their way to Hue. I would be taking a boat there about six months later. Quint led the way to the Cua Viet, since he had better navigation skills and was the senior petty officer. Being able to read a chart helped too. Now we could open up the boats and make some time as well. Our agreement was that he would get us lined up on the river entrance and we would try to pick our way through a few sandbars (that we were told were there) and find the channel. We did know that there was a YOG tied up to a big buoy a few miles offshore. They were pumping fuel to the small base, which would help us find the river entrance.

It was a nice little run and a few hours later we were beached at the little sand ramp and dropping our ramps to find out what was going on. There wasn't much there then, what later became known as Camp Kistler was a collection of plywood hooches, a few small bunkers, some RMK-BRJ employees, Marines for security and a little fuel bladder farm. The RMK guys were crewing a big dredge that was working its way upriver clearing a channel for boat traffic, for the bigger boats, we had a shallow draft and could run the river to Dong Ha. That's what the brass thought anyway.

For the first few days we didn't have much to do except make friends with the RMK guys and the Marines while moving in to a hooch. We cozied up with the RMK guys real fast! They not only had a small kitchen and a BBQ grill set up, but the Marines told us that these civilians could get us anything we wanted. They weren't lying; they had beer without preservatives in it and real booze! Hell, they even had a couple of refrigerators to go along with hot showers when the generator was on!

Our job was to work for everyone. We each had a big rubber 'bladder' unrolled in our well decks and we would haul fuel from the tank farm to refuel the dredge plus take it upriver for the Marines in Dong Ha. OSHA and the tree-huggers would have had a ball with this operation, where we loaded and unloaded it was a swamp of spilled fuel, both bladders leaked, the hose connections and pumps leaked and we left a trail of whatever we were hauling in the river.

NOTE

2005 Branson Missouri Reunion, on the fuel bladders. While talking with a few of the other Vets that had been involved in handling the fuel bladders, something interesting came up. Prior to our conversation I hadn't really thought about it too much, but in the beginning (up north) we didn't have 'cradles' for our fuel bladders.

The 'cradle' was a heavy wooden frame that held the bladder in a stationary position in the well deck. Like many things in the beginning no one thought about them. Our well decks were given a layer of sand to keep the bladders from resting directly on the track-cleats then they were just rolled out. One of the guys (in Branson) made the comment that, "Jesus Christ, that would have let the bladder move all over the place!"

Yep, he was right, they did. Although when the bladder was full it almost filled the entire 45' x 20' space in our well decks. They were rubber and filled with liquid. It made 'driving' the boats a little more interesting! Your cargo was almost always in motion.

When you turned the boat one way, it (the bladder) went the other way. The boat rolled with the change in weight distribution and wanted to make the turn harder...so you had to counter steer. The counter steering set the bladder moving back the other way and so on. You get the idea. On a forty-five minute to an hour trip (loaded), all you did was drive the boat, constantly! And, if you relaxed too much allowing the boat to sort of 'wallow' back and forth you could meet your other friend on the river, 'Mr. Sandbar'. Hitting a sandbar brought the boat to a very sudden stop...like hitting a wall.

Our first few trips were slow and cautious while we figured out where the channel went once we passed the dredge. After that was nailed we pretty much made as many loads as they wanted us to. Quint and I made two hand drawn charts of the channel in the river, compared notes both on the route to the ramp at Dong Ha and the route up another river to Quang Tri City. Just in case we had to go there for real someday, we did. We had no one in charge of us except for the Marines and they didn't care what happened as long as we did our job. It was quiet as far as 'Charlie' harassing us. During the first week we found out that we could run the river drunk as lords.

Cua Viet was also a different kind of place, one of the few places I can remember standing knee deep in water (while it's raining) and have sand blowing in your face. The entire area up there was made up of very fine sand, it was also almost constantly windy. As the wind shifted around the compass the sand was rearranged daily...okay, hourly, it seemed to always be in motion. This fine blowing sand found its way into everything. Your clothes, your hooch, your cot and blankets, your food, everything!

Just walking in it wore you out after a few yards, that's why all of the paths were made up of pallets and duck-boards.

Of course the good news was that there was no shortage of sand for filling sandbags. The other thing the sand was good for (as we would find out in the coming years) was saving lives. An enemy round landing in the soft sand would go in deeper before exploding, while the concussion of the explosion was about the same. Much of the shrapnel either blew upward or was slowed down by the sand.

The second week a typhoon began. Everything sort of turned a dull gray and stayed that way for about two weeks. When it wasn't raining, it was raining. If everything wasn't wet it was damp, other than the engine room of the boats (where we had a clothesline set up) the hooches were damp, the bunkers were damp, we were damp or soaking wet. Everything started to stink, grow mold and rot. I had been through another monsoon season, but in Da Nang, there you had a dry place to sleep and hot showers. Now our uniforms and our boots just rotted away and fell apart while we wore them!

As we became accustomed to the drastic change in temperature, our uniforms were modified to whatever cut-off pants we had - 'go-aheads' and flak jackets...no one that was in charge cared. We worked and partied.

Dong Ha and the Cua Viet River

One day the sun came out! Quint and his boat had been recalled for something else, you could only haul so much fuel anyway, we were alone and on that day for some reason had stopped drinking. This was probably a good idea to sober up for a while, but the entire crew getting sober on the same trip wasn't the best idea in the world.

On our second run of the day we were up past the dredge where the river split into five separate fingers. We had been running the river from memory; drunk or hung over and, in the rain. Suddenly I had no idea which of these fingers was the channel, worse neither did my crew! I brought the boat to a stop and we just sat there looking around and talking...no one knew where in the hell we should go! This was very embarrassing.

I have no idea how long we sat there trying to make a decision. I really didn't want to go back and get the chart we had so we tried to talk it out.

Shortly after, right about the time we were about to give up, a couple of mama-sans appeared in one of the little river skiffs and stared at us for a while. We stared back. Even at a hundred yards they would probably make out our confused expressions. They began waving and pointing to the one going to the left, we waved back and I began to follow that direction with some caution. Yep...it was the right one.

Scene at the ramp in Dong Ha, the old bridge is in the background, two Mike 8's in the foreground. The 918 is from the fleet so a ship out at sea was being unloaded. The nice paint job and fancy 'fender' (black thing near the bow) set it off as that. Source: Public domain.

The real build up was beginning about then. A few more boats arrived. U-Boats started showing up a few times a week bringing loads to the ramp at the Cua Viet end. The bladder was yanked out of my well deck so that we could haul the cargo upriver to Dong Ha. As the expansion really got going, I was pulled back to Da Nang. My boat was going to be overhauled, my crew was rotating back to the states and I had some papers to sign. Within a week, I had a new crew and was on a truck headed for Quint's boat south of Da Nang. Some other river that I had never heard of.

It was called the South Cau Dai River, in a place called 'The Arizona Territory'. We would refer to it just like the Marines did...Dodge City in the 'Arizona Territory'. In the future the LCM-8, 860, would become known as the 'Liberty Ferry', bridging a place on Highway 1 where the bridge would be blown up and washed out over the next few years, more than once or twice. Four Navy guys, one seventy-four foot boat and a bridge waiting to be built. In the middle of nowhere, protected by two platoons of Marines...surrounded by a very highly motivated bunch of Viet Cong.

Our call sign was also a joke back then. Someone, with an overworked sense of humor, came up with 'Blueberry Pie'.

Up to this point I only 'thought' I had been scared a few times. In the coming months I was going to get to know true, honest, total, absolute fear in a first-hand way. It would be my first time to think about giving myself a 'wound' to get out. It would also be the time I would consider 'fragging' an officer who was a total coward, but be smart enough not to do it.

Keeping My Boat While in Dong Ha, Late 1967

We had just pulled into the ramp at the mouth of the river and dropped the ramp on the boat. We had another trip to make that day so I left the engines at idle with the screws running slow. You did this and left someone at the helm so that the forklifts didn't push you off the beach when they ran in and out of your well-deck loading you.

As the first forklift headed for the boat with a pallet someone was walking down the ramp in our direction, I didn't pay much attention until he stopped by the ramp and signaled to me. Not having any idea what I had screwed up this time I walked up the gunwale and bent over by the bow, as the second forklift came up the ramp he cupped his hands around his mouth and yelled "Smitty wants to see you in Ops...right away".

The 'operations shack' in Cua Viet was just a little bit away from the ramp and set off toward seaside, a 'shack' it was not. Originally a metal shipping container measuring something like twenty feet by ten feet, it had grown in proportions, massive amounts of sandbags have that effect on anything. As the shelling up there had increased so had the amount(s) of sandbags we piled on everything. Through the sandbags on the roof, antennas bristled up all over it. This building housed our communications to everywhere our CO, Smitty and the radio operators worked it.

Hooches in the compound at Cua Viet.

How I Created the Problem

Every year or so our boats were sent back to Subic Bay in the Philippines for a major overhaul, in some ways this was good...in other ways it was bad, very bad! The guys working on these boats were just doing a nine to five job on an old landing craft (we figured) and didn't really know that the boat they were working on would be in combat once in a while. Now, every once in a while if you sent a really, really bad boat back, you got it back a little better. Sometimes, it was mostly a crap-shoot. You could almost count on sending back a boat that was running in top shape and all the equipment worked good on and then getting it back all screwed up.

Try this one. The boat goes back to Subic with bad screws and the ramp works well. When you get it back the ramp doesn't work, but it has two new screws. It also has two bent shafts and the packing glands leak like hell. So after you find this out you try to run cargo and fix the boat while your teeth get rattled out on every trip for a while. When you hit the beach/ramp you have to free-fall the ramp then, get a forklift to raise it again; if the air compressor or the air system wasn't fixed.

Smitty told me that the 913 was due for rotation, the new boat would arrive in the next few days and we should get ready to transfer our gear and take over the other boat as soon as it arrived. The only problem that my snipe and I saw with this was that the

913 was running like a new shiny dime, he had taken very good care of the boat. Everything worked very well for a change, the engines were in good condition, nothing leaked and the screws and shafts were good too. We talked about it, but the bottom line was that the 913 was going back.

I had been through this rotation shit before and didn't like it. We knew what we had now, so why change it? I did talk it over with the crew and the snipe said that we would take a look first before we changed boats, it made sense to me.

A few days later the boat arrived. We met up with the crew and introduced ourselves in one of the hooches. Jesus these guys were in dungarees and wearing white hats! They had standard Navy shoes and they were shined! We had a few beers and talked about the boat (if I remember it was the 576) and there were some problems they had noticed. This had to be the understatement of the year...noticed!

The one bank of engines seemed to smoke like hell most of the time. The steering wanted to lock up and was a little 'jerky', the engine controls didn't work right (they were sluggish and seemed too tight) and it wouldn't hold air pressure. The Bosun had tried to air start the engines and the air tank was completely empty after a few hours.

Me and my snipe went for a walk to get a better look at things. Yep, one side of the boat was covered with soot from the exhaust, the air gauge read zero, down below we saw that one set of engine control cables were smashed in their carriers, one packing gland for a shaft was seeping water. We went down into the after steering space and looked around too, the one steering ram was loose. We put our heads together then a little later got both of the crews together.

The solution was pretty simple. They could drink as much of our good booze as they wanted, same thing with the beer, they could have our best centerfolds and whatever else they wanted. While they enjoyed themselves, we had some work to do after dark.

They were taking the same boat back that they had delivered...no questions asked, it would just have different numbers.

I sealed the deal by opening up my locker and handing the bosun a sealed bottle of Jack Daniels. I told everyone else that the Cokes and beer were in the fridge and to enjoy.

We talked, drank and waited for the sun to set. Once it was dark the haze gray and white paint were ready to go, the next morning a very hung over crew followed a few U-Boats back to Da Nang...on the 576, leaving a beautiful trail of black smoke behind them in the still morning air.

We knew that it wouldn't happen in Da Nang, probably, but somewhere along the line the little mix up would be discovered. You see on one of the overhead beams in the engine room the boats serial number was written in welding. It sort of stood out like a sore thumb. We knew that we were going to be found out but had managed to keep the boat that was in the best condition a little longer.

When I walked into the ops shack, Smitty didn't even look up, the cigar was firmly clinched in his teeth, it just bobbed a little as he asked, "how's the 913 runnin'?" I answered that the 576 was running pretty good, the 913 was back in Subic. "You dickhead", he said still without looking up, "you switched numbers...you know damned well the 576 is in Subic."

Well I couldn't argue with that, it was the truth. So I just didn't say anything. Smitty took a deep drag on the cigar before looking up at me and exhaling. "I shoulda' been watchin' that little show of movin' shit around you peckerwoods put on that night. There's a fucking boat on the way up...you're gonna actually take this goddamned one...the 913 needs to go back for a goddamned refit...got it?"

Okay, I agreed. He had a way with words. Before I left I added, "As long as it runs pretty good."

He looked back down at the papers on his desk and said, "I can always get you a replacement if it doesn't, now...get the fuck out of here and haul some cargo."

I don't remember the boat number, but I do remember it was in pretty good shape. All we had to do was take the governors off of the engines to make it go faster and move all of our gear on board.

The Sadness of War

There have been numerous questions about this so, in this edition, I'll take the space to answer them. I mention, in the introduction, an incident with a sampan/Yabuta/bum boat, on the Cua Viet. It happened and, at the time, it was very sad and depressing to me. The complete waste of war is not a pretty thing.

It wasn't in our job description, but it was something we knew we had to do. It wasn't nice and it wasn't easy. I think about all of the truly innocent families, the ones just trying to survive from day to day, on the river, in this case the Cua Viet. When we had the time, the manpower – usually some Marines on board – we did a stop and search of boats on the river. We would have them stop and brought them alongside, pointed guns in their faces and demanded to see their papers. In many cases, we boarded and searched the boats, tearing a lot of stuff up for them.

We were looking for anything suspicious on the boat – guns, explosives, too much food and ammunition, anything that they could be transporting to aid the enemy. In isolated cases, they *were* transporting enemy troops; NVA or the guys in black pajamas.

What we didn't know, at the time, was that many were threatened into doing this. If they didn't, the bad guys would kill the entire family.

What we didn't expect and, rarely found, was an entire boatload of the enemy. Along with weapons.

That's what happened this time.

We were going up the river with a small load of palletized goodies of some kind. It was our second trip of the day. We had six or eight Marines aboard and things had been quiet for a while. I can't place it in a date, but I suspect that it was after Tet; things were a little 'tighter' after that happened and, we didn't trust anything or anyone. The interdiction became everyone's job, if you had the time.

The other thing that happened more and more were occurrences of blocking or herding our boats. By suddenly turning into your path or placing an innocent boat in it, they tried to get a boat to change course. In every case that this happened, the idea was to get the boat closer to a mine or, if they were lucky, get you to drive right over it. These were command detonated mines – there was someone sitting in the weeds, with the trigger, looking at the bamboo aiming stakes that were pushed into the ground.

The boats herded you close enough and, 'BOOM', the mine was triggered.

They knew where the mines were, we didn't. Sometimes the grappling hook on the sweep boat didn't catch the wire.

On this morning, as we approached an area where a lot of branches of the river converged, a boat almost the size of a Yabuta – about five or six meters long - came out of the one channel, from the north, then turned and started back in. It had a motor but it wasn't fast, there was enough water so I altered course and, cut it off. We brought it alongside.

The action of turning around and, appearing to run, made them look suspicious. Before they did that they were just another fishing boat.

Everyone knew the drill. You got a line on it and, while covering it with guns, said the words demanding papers and identification from everyone on board. They raised hell while you looked things over, you watched everyone on board, checked the papers and I.D.'s then did what you had to do.

I'd become pretty good at reading expressions, body language and posture; listening to voice tone and making 'people' assessments. Did they look at you or turn away, was someone trying to stay in the background – out of sight? There were things you keyed on. Also, scanning the visible areas of the boat for contents... some things created suspicion right away. Ages and dress of the passengers or people on the boat, too many big white bags of rice, too much of the contents covered with straw mats and other things, too heavy of a load of goods to be simple fishermen/family.

Everything about this boat was just very wrong. It fit most of what I wrote above as far as being suspicious as hell; right up to the twenty-something and very good looking girl handling the tiller in the stern of the boat.

On the Yabuta, there were people trying to stay hidden. The frantic level of the noise went up as we (now) demanded the papers and, were demanding that it happen very soon. There was just too much cargo and, too much of it was hidden, covered up and out of sight. There were also passengers who refused to show themselves...this is where the old stress level goes through the roof in a big hurry.

All of us had slipped the safety's off of our weapons and every muzzle was pointed at somewhere on the boat. It's one of those times that things suddenly slow down; everyone becomes very intense, extremely alert and just a little nervous. Stupidly, there were a few (on the Yabuta) who wanted to argue and scream rather than come up with anything resembling papers. No one was coming out of the shadows, no matter how many times we demanded it and, things were approaching the point of no return in a big hurry...a damned big hurry!

One of the Marines, off to my left, yelled 'GRENADE!' and, that was the end of it.

I didn't hear it bounce but, I caught the motion and saw it roll across a straw mat and bounce onto the floor of the boat. Was the pin pulled? We'll never know. Was the 'spoon' still on? Same answer – all we saw was a hand grenade rolling across the floor. In a space of time – a mere fraction of a second – the threat was accessed and, judged as just that. The stress and tension had led to that point; accented by the wild screaming and yelling from the people on the boat.

From what we were told later, they were transporting weapons and food. Within a few seconds that didn't enter into it. Once you pull the trigger there is nothing else and, at that range (maybe fifteen feet), no one missed. There was a lot of screaming...the girl at the tiller simply folded and went over backwards into the river...a few of the guys kept firing until they were empty. Most replaced their magazines and threw another round in the chamber.

My last sight of the girl was her standing up, both hands extended as if she was trying to signal 'stop'. The look on her face was one of pure terror...right before the rounds tore through her. No one wanted to go in after her; she just became 'debris' in the river.

We took the boat in tow, delivering it to security in Dong Ha.

We were all questioned about what had happened. No, the grenade didn't go off. It had been a tension-filled judgment call with a deadly outcome. However, what was found on the boat, pointed to everyone (on it) being either Viet Cong or, people working for them, in support. Our actions had been judged as 'justified'...incident closed.

Any way you cut it, it was a rotten way to start the morning.

The Ramp at Cua Viet Gets Destroyed

I had pictures of this destruction at one time – sent from a brother that I can't remember the name of. It looked as bad as it was.

As I remember, this happened in March of '68, by then the ramp at Cua Viet had grown to huge proportions. There was a major build up underway and the ramp was loaded with supplies and munitions. Every day the LCU's and YFU's arrived from Da Nang and made the run upriver to unload at the ramp at Dong Ha. At least every few days an LST would arrive and beach at the ramp at Cua Viet, we would stop hauling cargo from the ramp and get directly back loaded from the 'T' to get the stuff upriver and on to Khe San or Camp Carrol as quickly as possible. With only something like eight forklifts working the ramp the pace was pretty feverish most of the time, it was (on most days) a load and go situation, as soon as you had your load you ran the river. The first trip was made in convoy behind our mine sweepers but after that you were on your own; we ran the river wide open.

You called the ops shack on your radio and informed them that you were on your way upriver. If there was a problem somewhere you would just hang out for a while until you were cleared to go. Our job was to move as much cargo as possible every day and we did it well, seven days a week.

After all we did have a motto:

The Ramp at Cua Viet Gets Destroyed

'You call...we haul...rain snow sleet or Viet Cong.'

Well it didn't snow or sleet, but we did have the other two.

If your boat was loaded heavy (like two high pallets of 155 rounds), you sat back, put your one foot on the throttles, the other on the helm and kept it wide open pushing a lot of water all the way to Dong Ha. You kept an eye on the riverbanks and just wanted to make one more trip and survive it, along with everyone else on your crew.

Even with us running stuff up the river from daylight to dusk seven days a week, the stockpile at the Cua Viet ramp continued to grow at an amazing rate. Right after Tet we had begun to get loaded (the boats) following our return from our last river run. That way we were ready to go as soon as it was light enough to run the river...well, idle up the river behind our minesweepers.

It's funny now in some ways, I guess our brilliant military minds didn't think that the enemy would notice a mountain of ordinance piling up on the ramp. Not notice or try to take advantage of all of it in one nice compact area? This was the winter/spring of '68, the only way the area north of the river was anywhere secure is if there were Marines patrolling there, other than that it was a no-man's land.

Poor picture quality but it shows the beginning of the destruction of the ramp. This is looking inland (west) and up river. Our boats are long gone at this point and the really big ordinance is just beginning to cook-off. By ten am the fuel storage area was burning and, the cloud of smoke was about three times that size. Public Domain.

The morning everything blew up at Cua Viet (the first time) it was foggy as hell; you could just see the second boat beside you. There was an LST arriving as soon as the fog lifted, there were also a LCU and another Mike-8 stuck out there waiting. We were back loaded and ready to make our first run of the day, Ops wanted us to wait for it to clear a little then the minesweepers would lead as usual. We were all beached downriver from the ramp in a nice tight group, so close that you could walk from one boat to the other or hand things back and forth.

The standard uniform of the day was a pot, your flak vest, a pair of cut off jungle pants, skivvies (if you had them) and 'flip-flops', rubber shower shoes that we referred to as 'go-aheads'.

Most of us had fired up the engines, the ramps were up and we were drinking our canteen cup of C-Rats coffee while having the first cigarette of the day. The fog washed by keeping us nice and damp. My flak jacket was drenched in the dew from the fog. At this time of day you are apprehensive, nervous and it all becomes one emotion as you talk and crack a few tired jokes to try and ease the tension that everyone is feeling.

The Mike-6 minesweepers were slow and you think about following them all the way to the ramp at Dong Ha again, sitting ducks...once again.

Although loaded and pushed up on the beach in neutral, there is just a little bit of action in the water caused by the swells coming in from the South China Sea. As the boats rise and fall a few inches the exhausts burble when they go under and burp sending splashes of water up between the boats. You check gauges and look around giving someone else a good-natured ribbing about anything at all, trying to relieve your tension and theirs at the same time. You have waited too long to leave and the tension shows on everyone. It is dead calm and the odor of diesel exhaust hangs heavy in the air around all of us. A lot of the guys are checking weapons, ammo and getting ready for the trip. Others are squaring away the things that collect on the decks, sorting C-Rations and normal housekeeping. On a few of the boats the 'snipes' are in and out of the engine rooms checking things. Just a normal morning on the river.

The fog has lifted a little; you talk with your crew about anything and everything as you wait. None of it is important really, but you spend almost all of your days with these guys and each depends on the other. You are not friends, but you are in a strange way...for about a year. Most of the 'boat-drivers' are hanging out in the cons just waiting for the signal to move out and waking up. That's the time you check gauges, make radio checks and get your thoughts together before leaving, the ramps are up and locked.

I remember my snipe was working behind the con in the little area where the shelf was for cooking meals. He offered me a fresh cup of coffee. I handed my canteen cup over the back of the con to him.

I thanked him when the cup is full again and the extra pack of coffee is dumped in; there is a plastic spoon floating in it. Turning around I scan the gauges again and lean on the front of the con to look ahead. The beach is steep and the dune in front of the boats is a high one, sitting back from the dune a little are pallets of fifty-five gallon drums. They are piled two high and banded together, I have seen them sitting there for a few days.

I do remember two thoughts at that time: one was why were there drums of gasoline sitting there in the open (if they were filled with gas) and the other was wishing we could run the river in the fog, that way 'Charlie' couldn't see us?

About that time there was a short whistling sound that I am sure made everyone that heard it flinch, I know I ducked down as it went over! It was a 40 MM mortar round and if you heard it then it missed you, this was a little strange and I still wonder about this and the other thing that happened that morning, I don't ever remember old 'Charles' hitting us in the morning. Was he trying to hit the boats that morning, were there going to be more rounds after that one or did he have those drums 'dialed in' and knew what was in them? That single round landed right on those drums and my question about what was in them got answered with one hell of an explosion...yep it was gasoline!

There was a huge ball of flame as I don't know how many of the drums simply exploded when the round hit! Okay...time to haul ass! We had a mixed load of ordinance on that morning. Part of it was powder for big guns and that had just happened about thirty feet in front of my boat...see 'ya guys. All of a sudden everyone was wide awake, there was no communication with anyone as we scrambled, throttles pulled all the way back to get off the beach and into the river! Being this close to each other and backing down in a hurry the old tires that we hung over the sides of the boats for 'fenders' would squeal as they rubbed the other boats, when two made contact they would flip up in the air sending out a shower of water.

We got into the channel and milled around a little waiting and holding our own against the slow moving current, there were a few other things blowing up while we waited but now we were far enough away. In a few minutes there was a huge ball of fire and it was growing quickly, more of the drums exploded we could see stuff flying and some ammo started to cook off too, there were no more rounds from the other side of the river. The fog was beginning to lift and you could see almost a hundred feet all around you. There was a short communication with the Ops shack and we were told to get the hell out of there! You didn't have to tell us twice! We were pretty much told to just run the river, no minesweeper or anything just get to Dong Ha and stay there until we were told to return to base.

Those guys with that mortar had to be very happy with themselves!

I was probably the third or fourth boat back as our convoy headed out. Two miles upriver (and one sandbar later) the fog cleared and we were back enjoying another bright sunny day in paradise. It was a very nice day as we ran the river as fast as we could! We didn't mind not having the mine sweeper leading us; the reason was that (even loaded) we were faster and if Charlie was sitting along the river waiting to trigger a mine it would probably be a 'miss'. We at least hoped that. The other thing was that if you were shot at they had to 'lead' a moving target and we tried to move fast.

What happened next was sort of strange and I still wonder about this, like I said above. Was this blind luck or did Charlie really know how long it took for us to run the river and he was just a little 'early' that day? Was it his intention to flush us out of Cua Viet, and then pound us when we were all unloading at Dong Ha?

Modern day ramp at Dong Ha. Author's picture.

Busy morning sometime in 1967. Public Domain.

Coming around that last right turn before the ramp at Dong Ha, everyone came to a stop. We were under a half mile away from the ramp when the two lead boats pulled up. I remember being alongside a guy whose nickname was 'Flip' while we sat there waiting looking upriver then at each other; there was enough engine noise that we couldn't actually hear them (the rounds) going off, but we could feel the explosions.

What we had was becoming a very nasty situation; flushed out of Cua Viet, stopped dead in the water like targets (now),waiting for things at the Dong Ha ramp to clear. We could get shot at here or maybe pounded once we landed...not good at all.

While we sat there in the bright morning sunshine the ramp was getting pounded by 'Charlie' and the river was filled with geysers from exploding rounds! Although it only lasted a few minutes it was intense. It seemed that most of the rounds were landing in the river right off the ramp. Right where we should be parked.

Five more minutes and all of us would have been right under that...damn!

There was so much confusion, at both ends of the river now, that there was no communication at all with us. Once things quieted down we approached the ramp with extreme caution landed and the fork lift drivers started to unload us, everyone was very jumpy, we wanted to be empty and gone as soon as possible. Like everyone else I spent a lot of time glancing at the river behind the boat. And, I didn't think we were going anywhere for a while, at least not today.

A few of us went to talk to the officer in charge of the ramp operation, we were told that the ramp at Cua Viet was one big mess and that we were probably trapped upriver for a while. We didn't want to hear that, but he was right.

That single round had set off a huge gasoline fire, as more of the drums of gasoline exploded the fire had spread to piles of staged ordinance all around. This was a chain reaction that just went on and on...and on. There had been no real way to fight the initial fire (even though we were told that everyone tried) and as everything just got out of control the ramp was simply abandoned while everyone took cover.

Ammunition of all kinds was cooking off and flying in all directions after the first few minutes, everything from small arms ammo to hand grenades, flares and mortar rounds. The area was also stuffed with 155/175 mm artillery rounds powder (for the guns) and fuses, when that stuff started going off it had to be absolute hell! The other piece of not-so good news was that some of the stuff had been tossed into the 'bladder-farm' beside the ramp. Adding to the excitement was something like 50,000 gallons of diesel fuel and JP-4 burning too, that's what was making the huge cloud of gray/black smoke we had been watching.

We just sat and waited. We could see a huge cloud of smoke rising from there and with the boats shut down could hear some occasional big explosions. Old 'Charles' must have been really proud of himself that morning, that one little mortar round costing maybe five bucks managed to destroy hundreds of thousands of dollars in material.

A little later, here comes our minesweeper!

And not alone. The boys are leading a small convoy of U-Boats! We moved away from the ramp to give them room enough to land, then while they are getting unloaded went to talk to the crews. They had stayed as far to the north side of the channel as they could while passing the ramp and it had been fun, they were above decks at battle stations while stuff was falling in the water all over the place. They confirmed the information we had been given that the ramp was blowing up all over and the fuel dump was burning...yep we were stuck.

While they could get unloaded and head back for Da Nang (if they felt like running past the ramp again) our 'home' was blowing itself up! We sort of relaxed and spent that day and the night waiting for things to die down and hoping we could return in the morning. The last place we wanted to spend another night was at Dong Ha! Yes, the U-Boats did head home after unloading.

We were also just a little nervous after that nice warm 'reception' that had probably been intended for us in the morning. During the night we kept watching the fireworks in Cua Viet. It did decrease in intensity after a while except for the occasional flash of something cooking off.

The crew on the new Mike-8 wasn't exactly happy to be there either. It was one nice warm welcome to a new area.

By the next morning we were told that we had permission to return to the mouth of the river...after the mine sweeper got to us.

It was a mess. The LST was beached at the ramp and they were ready to begin back loading us as soon as the first boat was at the ramp. There were piles of debris pushed up all over the place a lot of stuff was still smoking and they were pouring water on everything that was still warm (which was most of it). Everyone still looked pretty shocked and, worn out. There were the remains of burned up forklifts and a crashed helicopter on the other side of the watchtower; we were told that they had tried to pull a medevac at night. The blades had clipped a telephone pole and everyone was killed.

Our hooches had taken some damage. There was no water and the generator was out. They didn't want us doing too much walking around because there was still live ordinance of all kinds lying around all over the place and it hadn't been rounded up yet. We had a choice of getting off the boat and standing by it or staying on the boat, most of us just stayed on the boats.

It took a few days to finally get everything cleaned up and I don't think there was that much stuff staged at Cua Viet ever again. And us? You guessed it; we were back living on the boats. It took days of clean-up before we were allowed to even check out our damaged hooches.

After writing that chapter, I ran across one of the forklift operators that had been working in Cua Viet. The pictures were sent by him as well as the newspaper clipping that describes what happened to the folks at home. Funny, it's not even slightly accurate…well maybe in the sense that the ramp was totally destroyed? That part is accurate. It also helped me remember the date.

I also learned in the past few years that no one but 'Charlie' learned anything from this. It seems that in late 1968 (after I was out of country) our guys did the same thing. There was a massive build-up of ordinance again, on the same ramp. The next time it was a short rocket attack that got the party started. Ok, so the second time the bad guys spent a little more money maybe, they had just as much fun watching it go up I'm sure.

The Two Questions

"Were you scared?" and the Million Dollar question.

Think about the one time in your life that you were scared out of your wits, the one time that you were so hopelessly, totally scared that you were either positive that you wouldn't live past it or you thought about that in a brief moment (if your brain had the time) and released everything your bladder held.

Yes...we were all scared out of our wits at one time or another, sometimes more than once in the same day, you just tried not to think about what 'might' happen. Other times you were pretty positive that you were going to die. You may get an answer.

"Did you ever kill anyone?" That is what's called the Million Dollar Question, the one question that you never ask anyone that has been in combat at all...never.

If you make the mistake of asking that question he probably won't bother to answer you and the conversation is over. Your answer will be to have his eyes go very strange before he turns and walks away from you, probably to never speak to you again.

If, on the other hand, his answer is a glowing response about a battle: you just got yourself a pencil-pusher that was in a rear area. They always want to talk about it.

We Prove Just How Stupid We Are One Night...and Live Through It

I don't remember exactly when this happened, but at the time there were at least eight Mike-8's stationed at Cua Viet. It was after the death of 'Frosty' Cain (August '67) in Hue, I was transferred back to the Dong Ha river to take over the 876 boat; its skipper was rotating back to the 'world'. The Marines were in the middle of some major operations in our area and north toward the DMZ, it seemed that almost every night B-52's were pounding the area around the DMZ, even miles south the exploding bombs in the DMZ made the ground shake, there were constant firefights, flares and tracers all around us most nights.

We were getting a little worn out after a while. Our unit was providing the main supply route for anything in the re-supply chain. If an LCU didn't take it to the ramp at Dong Ha, an LST dropped its cargo at the ramp at Cua Viet, that's as far as the (bigger) ship could go. We would then be backloaded with whatever they had and deliver it upriver to the ramp at Dong Ha. Our boats ran seven days a week, eight to ten hours a day, we were getting worn out because not only were we being harassed on that twelve mile river run during the day but the nights weren't a lot better. If 'Charlie' wasn't throwing the occasional round in just to make sure we were paying attention he was probing the perimeter of the Marines or, the 155MM mobile gun battery was firing at some target. We had pretty nice hooches, but spent a lot of time in the bunkers beside them.

The other things making our lives interesting were the big guns 'Charlie' had hidden in caves on the other side of the DMZ (Demilitarized zone).

There were mountains near the coast that had caves in them. Apparently old 'Charles' had guns that could be rolled out when he was in the mood to have some fun with us. At this same time there were destroyers and the battleship New Jersey that ran fire missions up and down the coast. Most of the time the guns stayed in the caves because of these ships. He ('Charlie') had a habit of rolling them out at night for a little while and throwing a bunch of rounds at us to amuse himself, by the time the ships got the fire mission and were on station to return fire they were back in the caves probably laughing and playing cards, the ships would pound them for a while then quit.

What we couldn't ever figure out was why all of the ships went to re-supply at the same time...they always did it at night? Before they were even out of sight, 'Charlie' was rolling the guns out and getting ready to have some more fun with us. It got to the point that when we realized the ships were leaving we would just go sleep in the bunkers. We had learned from experience that it wouldn't be long until the first round was on the way.

Even in the bunker it was still hard to get a decent night's sleep, just because of the noise all around outside and the tension you felt.

The bunkers had rats living in them and smelled like hell.

The weather was pretty nice for a change (so it almost had to be in the spring after the monsoon season) and after a while a few of us put our heads together and came up with a plan for a little peace and quiet. As you read this you will begin to wonder what we were thinking...trust me we weren't thinking straight at all.

The idea we came up with was that we would all go to a nice wide spot in the river a few miles up from the base camp at Cua Viet; we picked an area that was flat and cleared on both banks. We would all nest together (in the middle of the river) for the night and ride on one anchor. We would post watches and tie up loosely so that if anything happened we could get away. For some reason this sounded so good that even Smitty (the NCO in charge of us) agreed to it and got the 'old mans' approval. To this day I still can't believe that they went along with this idea.

As dusk began to settle, we put any extra gear aboard the boats that we needed and headed upriver. It was a very nice night. I seem to remember a completely cloudless sky and there was almost no wind. Reaching the area, we tied the boats up so that four of each was stern to stern and four abreast. It was a nice little floating group riding a single anchor in a calm river. Darkness fell as we assigned watches, checked weapons and handled anything else that needed to be taken care of for the night. Except for movement on the boats, a little quiet talking and the occasional sound of a pop top, a rubbing line or fender, it was pretty quiet. Most of us were pretty relaxed and looking forward to getting a good night's sleep. I would bet that most of us were not wearing our flak jackets or pots, as I remember someone called the ops shack and told them we were settled in.

Before it was totally dark 'Charlie' started his nightly crap. We watched flares in the distance, occasional bunches of tracers as they bounced off in all directions in the night sky and mixed heavy fire. You could always tell who was firing at whom at night with the heavy machine guns, our tracer ammunition burned red; the ones of the enemy were either green or white. Near the mountains west of Dong Ha, we also watched a Dragon ship tearing the hell out of 'Charlie' for a good while. I was always amazed at the stream of tracers that poured to the ground like liquid fire. It was so quiet that we could hear the muted roar of the Gatling guns. Between that low growling roar and the stream of tracers, that's how the Dragon ships got named. We should have been paying better attention then, we would have heard 'Charlie' and his buddies laughing their butts off on the north shore.

It had to be rough for them, convulsed with laughter and trying to plan our little party that evening at the same time?

We, Einstein's all, failed to realize that our plan had a few major flaws in it, so big that you could drive a battleship through them.

First, eight of us going upriver before dark to the same area on a nice quiet night, that's about as subtle as a plane crash!

Then, even if 'Charlie' didn't realize what was going on right away when all of the engines were shut down in the same area, wouldn't that give something away...? Naaaaaaw, guess we didn't think so. Did we think that someone watching near base wouldn't notice all of us dummies going upriver?

Maybe pass the information on? Nope not us.

Oh...one other little thing, the boats are all tied together, loose, but still tied. Uh, none of us rocket scientists thought there would maybe be a problem untying them in total darkness and under a little bit of stress? Again, nope.

The only thing we forgot to do was put up the big billboard that said 'Shoot at us...We're stupid!' the one with the flashing lights.

We settled in for the night, set the first watch and someone was playing a radio real low on one of the boats. Anyone that was smoking was doing it in either a well deck or below decks. When we did have time to listen to a radio the station of choice was the one in Hanoi, there was North Vietnamese propaganda broadcast to try and demoralize us but in the evenings 'Hanoi Hanna' also played some real good mixes of rock and roll with a little protest music thrown in. We ignored the propaganda and enjoyed the music, it was much better than Armed Forces Radio anyway.

Just about the only intelligent thing I did before sacking out in the con was to double check the stop buttons for the engines, I made sure they were pushed down all the way. If and when it was time to start them all I had to do was either push the buttons for the air or the electric starters and they were running. I wrapped myself in a couple of those nice scratchy woolen Navy issue blankets found a soft spot on the wooden floor of the con, used my flak jacket for a pillow and prepared for a good night's rest. God...we all needed it!

I don't know how long I laid there before I started to drift off to sleep but probably not long. I remember hearing the guys on watch having a hushed conversation. The river was hardly moving at all so about all there was for noise was the fighting going on in the distance a little 'arty' once in a while and the little bit of noise from the gentle easy movement of the boats.

Then, in the distance I heard this real strange little sound. It was sort of a combination of a 'thump' and a 'whoosh'. It's really hard to describe the sound, it also sounded far away, but close at the same time if that sounds sane? In a second or two that sound was followed by another one.

We Prove Just How Stupid We Are One Night...and Live Through It

Well, at least I didn't have to lay there in suspense all night and wonder what the sound was.

Yep...our buddy 'Charles' wanted us to feel right at home no matter where we were on the river...it was a 121MM rocket, actually not just one. HE HAD A WHOLE DAMNED TRUCKLOAD OF 'EM!

Christ, in seconds it was raining rockets all around us, I mean this was like the monsoon season of rockets!

There could be a sound that is more memorable than the one these babies make on the way in, but I doubt it. It's a screaming, tearing sort of ripping combination that really wakes you up. I don't know if that rocket was designed to make that sound or it was just a happy accident, but it made your skin crawl! The explosion of the warhead was a very sharp loud 'CRACK'.

Before the first one hit the water, thirty-two idiots were up and moving!

I rolled out of the blankets and wound up on my knees in front of the control panel, pushing on the start buttons to roll the outboard engine on each bank. As soon as they fired I pushed the engine controls into forward (engaging the transmissions that linked them) and pulled the other two in. This technique was pretty much an assumed emergency start procedure on one of these boats. In around five seconds you had almost fifteen hundred horsepower growling under your feet and ready to go to work. Well, in this case, under my knees and the screws were turning!

I remember yelling to get us untied, as did a few other boat-drivers and in seconds boats were firing up all around me...yep, it was pretty much general panic.

While rockets blew up all over the place, shrapnel whizzed by and slammed off the sides of the boats. W flew into action with what I am sure had all of the grace of a Three Stooges movie. I have no idea how the line handlers got most of the boats untied as engines roared to life all around. I'm pretty sure there was some knife work involved and I do remember still being tied up with another boat and going around in circles before we finally broke the line to the anchor. It still amazes me that we even managed to get loose! The only way I can come close to describing the feeling, just how much total confusion there was at that moment would be to use the phrase 'absolute terror' then take it to a power of something like ten.

Even with all of the confusion going on, it was easy to spot our base at the mouth of the river, imagine that...damn they were under attack too! Not only were they trading rounds with 'Charles', but on the Marine side of the compound there were flares hanging in the air, star shells bursting all over the place and tracers bouncing off into the night sky at all angles. Yep, they were having fun too and it would probably go on for a while.

We had done a very good job of trapping ourselves. We weren't going upriver to Dong Ha in the dark...we couldn't stay where we were and chances were that we weren't going to the base, there wasn't really a 'list' as far as options just then. We couldn't just hang out on the river all night either, our little brown buddies would just find another way to amuse themselves with us even if they were out of rockets.

My 'snipe' was in the con with me as we ran down the river wide open, the seaman and engineman had untied us from the other boat and were standing around outside of the con. We were all pretty well shaken up, but no one was hurt.

The radio was clogged with a lot of chatter, but someone gave Ops a call anyway to let them know what was going on and tell them we were on our way back. We were told to keep going sea side and bypass the ramp, there was an YOG (small fuel ship) out there tied up to the fueling buoy. "Stay there tonight!" Smitty told us.

As we drove by, they were indeed getting the hell kicked out of them. There was a lot of ordinance landing on the ramp area. Our PBR (small river patrol boat) was engaged in a little firefight on the north bank of the river near a spot called Jones Creek. There were flashes of exploding rounds in the area of our hooches, in the area that the Marines occupied and the entire 'kill zone' in front of their perimeter was fully illuminated with flares floating down slowly on parachutes and illuminating the area with their reddish-pink glow. The area was so lit up that we had no trouble finding the channel leading to the sea. We kept our heads down, the throttles wide open and ran past the ramp and no one turned any running lights on until we were well out of the river. That was probably the only smart thing we did that day.

The amazing thing was that no one on any of the boats even had a scratch after all of that! We were all shaken up and probably had a heart rate that was up around a thousand, but that was it. Ops got a hold of the YOG to let them know that we were on the way and with a lot of relief we tied up alongside of it for the rest of the night. We were also famous for a while as the entire small crew of the little tanker turned out to greet us.

This tanker stayed moored to a big buoy about two miles off of the coast, it pumped fuel and gas to our tank farm. They could sit there and watch what was going on, but didn't know what it was like; they were pretty safe out there. Once we were tied up alongside we were feeling safe too and coming off of a real adrenaline rush!

It was quite a contrast, these guys were aboard a real 'ship' in the real navy and wore the real standard Navy uniforms. The lower rates were in dungaree uniforms with white hats and polished shoes, they were neat and clean, we hadn't seen ironed uniforms and shined shoes in months.

Then, here come the 'River-Rats'.

Our 'uniforms' were way beyond relaxed. We normally dressed in something that resembled whatever we had to wear that day. While some us had remnants of Marine (field) uniforms, most of our pants are cut off and we are mostly bare-chested except for our thread-bare flak jackets. We are wearing either combat boots or 'flip-flops', there are a few guys that are in civilian shorts or swim trunks. For the most part we wore nothing that designated our rank. Some of us were a little shaggy because we haven't had a haircut or a shave in a while, we have some guys with beards and the guys on the tanker are neatly trimmed and polished.

I would also bet that at least one of us was wearing one of those gaudy flowered Hawaiian tourist shirts, we all had one or two of them and you wore it under your flak jacket of course.

As far as our 'uniform' dress is concerned, we are about as far from the 'real' Navy as you can get...there is one thing...we live there at the mouth of the river and have won a unit commendation medal for our 'uncompromising performance in the face of hostile action'. We run cargo on the river eight to ten hours a day, seven days a week, no matter what happens.

We Prove Just How Stupid We Are One Night...and Live Through It

We were also about to pull our second collective stupid-as-hell stunt within twenty-four hours. We were on a roll that day and by God we were not going to quit until we had done it right!

The guys on this little tanker didn't get out much and they only had limited liberty. When in Saigon, while we lived here, they wanted to know what it was like so we sat around and told some 'sea stories' for a while. A 'sea story' is the Navy's version of a fairy tale; the main difference between the two is that instead of 'once upon a time' a 'sea story' begins with the words 'now this ain't no shit'. And, watched our base get hammered by 'Charlie'. On board the tanker the only weapons they had were a couple of fifty's by the bridge, the guys standing watch were carrying old M-1's and forty-five caliber pistols, they were fascinated by the varied array (and amount) of weapons we had on the boats. That and the 'personal' weapons we carried, most of us had some kind of a sidearm, as well as a fully automatic weapon. At this time I wore a cut-down 30 caliber carbine like a very long pistol.

We had a lot of other 'toys' that fascinated them too. Some of us had a few LAWs (light anti-tank weapons like a short bazooka) hanging around, assorted hand grenades and other goodies we had accumulated over time. The magazines for our weapons were either taped together in two's or three's so you didn't have to hunt around for another one after you emptied the first one.

We had cases of ammo for our weapons within easy reach. After all you don't take a knife to a gun fight; we wanted to be able to get to it in a hurry.

When the officers and higher rated petty officers started to turn in, we broke out the booze (forgetting that the last time these guys may have had a beer was probably a month ago) and partied for a while.

They also had a galley to raid so it worked out pretty well. The ice machine was quickly emptied to fill up our coolers. Well, you have to have cold beer right?

In exchange for cold cuts, fresh cheese, bread and some fruit, we traded cold beer, drinks and shots of black market whiskey; we also passed around a few good joints as we drank. While we came down from our adrenaline rush and got nice and 'mellow', the guys on the YOG got completely wasted and we didn't even realize it. Hell for us this was a normal evening on the river!

I don't know when we all went to bed, but the gentle swell in the South China Sea sort of rocked us to sleep. The next morning everything was a little hazy, not the weather, my brain. Since we knew that we had to get back and load for our first trip upriver we just thanked the guys on watch slipped our lines and hauled ass in the morning. After our first trip most of us were back at the ramp getting backloaded when Smitty walked down and summoned the craft commanders to join him. He was a nice enough guy, but he never smiled too much. Right now he wasn't smiling at all and the normal cigar in his teeth was clenched in there pretty tight. He was pissed about something and waited for us to gather around before beginning his speech.

"You're a sorry bunch of assholes!" he began as he looked us all over. Smitty had been a Bosun's mate for quite a few years and was another guy that could put an entire sentence together with exquisite profanity while chewing ass without even raising his voice above the normal conversation level. Like most born leaders, he was a master of the ass-chew. While raising his voice just enough to be heard over a passing forklift, he got his message for the day across to us.

"You 'peckerwoods' forgot you were tied up to a 'real' ship last night, didn't you?"

"I set it up so that you frigging idiots could go tie up out there every night for a while and get some R&R."

For the next few minutes he explained that he had spent a lot of time on the radio with the captain of the YOG…saving our asses. The captain didn't appreciate most of his crew being either drunk on duty, totally stoned or waking up so hung over that they couldn't make morning muster. He wanted all of us punished in some way and Smitty had really worked this time to keep us from going to a Captains Mast as a group.

After letting this sink in for a minute he said, "If any of you goddamned morons go anywhere near that frigging YOG again…ever (pause) ever…without specific (pause) goddamned orders…he's probably gonna goddamned shoot you…and I'll load the goddamned frigging gun!"

Again he paused to let that sink in, then, "Get your sorry asses upriver."

As we turned to leave he stopped us. "Hey, anyone got a bottle of decent Scotch?" There were replies of a few different brands and he picked one asking that it be delivered to the Ops bunker. "How about beer, anyone have anything good?" I had hauled beer last and had the most on board, so I offered up the selection. He thought about it then said, "Okay…have one of your guys bring up two cases of the Fall-flat." That was what we called Falstaff beer. It didn't matter, that would leave my boat with something like thirty cases until we had another load to break into.

It could have been worse. 'Charlie' could have had the range right with the first few rockets. And, 'Smitty' was still on speaking terms with us.

Something as Important as a Can Opener

Our meals consisted of C-rations (C-Rats) most of the time while on ops. In the beginning we were eating ones packed at the end of World War 2. I guess the idea was that these should be used up first before we got the new ones. By the time I left for the last time, we had eaten our way to 1957! We did supplement our meals with some real food, most of us bought or traded with the Vietnamese that we could trust for what they had to sell, in times of relative calm we also 'hunted' for chickens and loose pigs.

Yes, we went hunting for real. There were a few destroyed abandoned villages around Cua Viet and there were animals running loose in the bush all around us. In one way we also provided a service for the Marines in the compound. On their perimeter they had Claymore mines set up as well as trip-flares to illuminate the 'kill zone', this little mine blew a mass of fragments in one direction as a countermeasure. They set some up on trip-wires and many nights our sleep would be disturbed when a pig would trip one of these mines or a flare.

If enemy activity was low, we would get permission to go hunting for a while. Normally we would have one guy with a lower caliber weapon that would do the shooting. Everyone else would have heavier automatics to serve as security just in case.

Something as Important as a Can Opener

There was also an arrangement (with the locals) at the ramp at Dong Ha for meals. Depending on how many of us were there a few boats would come over from the north side of the river. They would have prepared meals in stacked tin containers for sale; most of the food they sold us was very good. Every meal contained lots of rice some kind of meat (which we never questioned species of) or fish, greens and veggies. They were good and they were warm. When we finished the meal we would signal them, they would come back and pick the empty containers up, it was a good system. We also knew that when they weren't around something was probably going to happen. These people would also gladly sell us chickens, fish and pigs sometimes; you had the choice of buying them 'kicking' or ready to cook and serve.

When we were in a time of not being able to do any of the above for food, it was back to the C-Rats. Don't get me wrong, these meals were probably healthy and nourishing, but after twenty plus years in a can they left a lot to be desired as far as 'taste' went. The can openers packed with the meals were referred to as a P-38, this little folding can opener was as much an important part of daily life as your boat or your helmet. How important? So important that when you found a good one you put it on the chain with your dog-tags until it was worn out.

Again, some genius had thought of this when they invented the P-38, it had a hole in one end that your chain fit through perfectly. They were designed so that when you flipped it open or closed it sort of locked in place. I don't know about other guys, but I decided mine was worn out when it would open by itself and stick me in the chest in the middle of the night. Ouch.

This was before they figured out how to keep the oil and peanut butter together. When you opened a can it was a chore to stir the oil back into the congealed mass below it. If you didn't soften the peanut butter up a little it turned a cracker (also in a little can) to powder when you tried to spread it.

Chow time was a study in barter finesse and one-upmanship that you could probably write a whole book about. It became more heated and serious when the C-Rats were getting low. You see there were just some of these meals that we couldn't bear to eat, not that they were bad or anything they just were not appetizing even to look at. We lived and worked together like any good boat crew, but even I was not above trying to pull rank on a seaman for a better meal. I say trying because when things got lean I got told to 'go to hell' with a smile. Like the Ham and Lima Beans meal, you had to be bordering on starvation to even think about eating that!

There was very little ham in it and it didn't even really look like real ham. The lima beans were all sort of a pasty looking off white to sometimes a little greenish color; this was packed in a sort of whitish gooey sauce. Heating it didn't really help much; I tried once and tossed it over the side after a few bites.

I also believe that at some time there was a poll taken, either that or an officer was forced to eat one of the ham and lima beans meals just once. In the 'newer' rations that meal came up missing!

So what did we do with the meals we didn't eat? They got stripped of all the good stuff, like the cigarettes and peanut butter and jelly crackers, the P-38 and the utensils then re-packed. Why? On a lot of trips on the river there would be places that we were close to a village, as the boat approached there would be a bunch of kids appear and run along the riverbank begging for anything. Every so often we would throw some of the good stuff, most of the time they got the ham and lima beans or pork and beans.

I can just imagine the disappointment of a poor little Vietnamese kid (that is actually eating better chow than you are) running down the river bank with his buddies waving and yelling 'GI...GI!' and motioning you to throw him something (thinking it might be candy?). A couple of us start tossing cans and they actually try to catch them as a group, yep, like a bunch of infielders going for a fly ball.

Most of the time it had to hurt, I mean the collisions, the missed catches and the next can whacking one or more of them had to be bad enough! You scramble for it, get all dirty and draw blood (taking a few lumps on the way) for an olive drab eight ounce can of ham and lima beans. Now that I think about it maybe the kids were mining the rivers to get even with us for that.

Card Sharks

In the forward areas there wasn't much to do for recreation. In Chu Lai we actually had an enlisted man's club that was pretty nice. We also had some time to throw some baseballs and footballs around when we had them. Cua Viet was all sand, in our little compound we put down 'duck boards' and old pallets to walk on, we never had a club but we had informal hooch groups.

When we weren't writing a letter home, reading or just relaxing, we would gravitate to a hooch where your immediate friends were to talk, drink a little and sit in on the inevitable card game. Most evenings there was some kind of a card game going on somewhere.

While we were living on the LSD in Da Nang harbor, the big game was Gin Rummy. It seemed like everyone played Gin and it was always played for money. When you were all broke or close to it the stakes went down, after payday they went back up again. I got pretty good at the game and always had a little stash put aside for my card playing money.

When we moved to the APL, the game changed to Pinochle for some reason and after a while you could wander into the mess area (when there wasn't a meal going on this is where everyone hung out) and there would be a few games going on. I had learned to play the game while in boot camp, but now it became something serious with us.

I had never played it for money. These guys were fond of playing a cut-throat version of the game either with three or four players and no one ever partnered up. Everyone played the game with a sense of humor and I don't remember anyone getting mad seriously, there was the usual ass busting, ribbing and general name calling, but it was all just in fun.

If I wanted to play, I had to learn the game and learn it well. Most of the time we played penny a point, dollar a hand and five dollars a 'set'. I enjoyed playing the game, but now stood the chance of dropping twenty or thirty dollars in one game. It was a real learning experience for a nineteen-year-old. It was also a challenge that managed to keep you from getting bored.

The guys played in a serious, but good natured way.

I got good enough that my stash of card money stayed about even while we were living there. Oh sure I did have some winning periods. but getting in a game with the wrong players could change that in one evening.

This all changed after a while in Cua Viet. When I went there for the second time it had built up more. There were more boat crews, since we could only operate during daylight hours our evenings were free. Most days we didn't make a run upriver after four or five o'clock, you got back loaded pushed the boat up on the beach hard and you were done for the day.

You ate, grabbed a shower (if the line wasn't too long) and then thought about socializing for the evening. The poker game of choice in Cua Viet was Acey-Deucey.

This was another fun but serious poker game that could go on for quite a while to finish just one hand. I haven't played the game in something like thirty years, but one rule stands out, in order to stay in the game and bet you had to match the 'pot'. This wasn't bad early in the game, but as the pot grew sometimes you were matching a few hundred dollars, then more, then more again.

This quickly separated the boys from the girls!

There were a few of us that were constant winners. After all, the game was all luck and some bluffing. You also learned when to fold just like any other poker game. After a few months I not only had a stash of 'funny money' in my hooch, but a box of it on the boat, no one messed with anyone else's belongings so there was no fear of theft in either place.

The hooch's where we congregated usually had a refrigerator and it was filled with beer, what else were they for? You had your friends, a good game and cold beer. The only thing that would screw up a nice evening was our friend 'Charlie'. He had a habit of waiting until a game was going real well, then throwing in a few rounds to break it up. We'd grab our cards and run for the bunkers. When it looked like it was safe we went back to the game.

Of course if it was big stuff coming in we didn't grab anything but our pots and flak vests! If it went on too long we'd divide the pot up before hitting the sack. It was only fair.

There was one other rule about the game that could be good or bad depending on the outcome and your hand. When the pot grew to over two thousand dollars, the hooch was 'locked down' until the hand ended. No one was allowed to enter or leave. The only way this rule was broken was if 'Charlie' decided to break the game up.

I do remember one night that I learned to hate that rule.

The game started out sort of slow with no big pots, none of us were playing well and it seemed that there was no one riding a hot streak that night. There were five of us playing and a lot of watchers in the hooch. Play went on for a few hours and the winnings remained pretty much evenly distributed among the players. In the last hand this changed.

I was dealt the winning hand straight up. I don't even remember what it was now, but boy did I know it that night!

The pot quickly built to two thousand dollars and the hooch was 'locked down' as always. As we played on the other, three players had to fold due to lack of funding. Now you couldn't 'borrow' from the pot and others in the hooch couldn't help finance you, even if you did have the winning hand. This was straight-up on your own poker.

It came down to me, a guy named John Cohen and a pile of MPC in the middle of the table. Neither of us knew how much money the other had, but we were playing in his hooch. I matched the pot and had a friend begin to count and divide my remaining cash into bundles of hundreds. John was bluffing, but matched it with no problem. All he had to do was walk to his wooden locker and bring back a box of MPC.

The pot was over four thousand dollars and I was 'short'. Even though there was a box of MPC on my boat, it wasn't going to do me any good right now. I don't recall everything that I was thinking besides probably absolute disdain over that rule and...probably hoping for just one round from 'Charlie' about then. Now I didn't whine about it, but I tried to get the rule bent a little.

Well, I wound up folding. John didn't have to show his hand, but he did with a broad smile and he had been bluffing his ass off. He had nothing! I turned my cards over and just banged my head on the table while a few gasps came from the watchers. The sure fire winner had been suckered and I learned a very important lesson that night.

A few weeks later things did even out with some help from 'Charlie'.

We had been having the usual card game in the same hooch and it was going pretty well. I was winning a little along with a few other guys and we were having a fun evening of friendship, beer and Acey-Deucey. There was a pretty nice pot building, but since I didn't have a decent hand I had dropped out to let that one finish. Going for a beer while I waited, suddenly we all heard the chilling sound of a 121mm rocket coming in. I forgot the beer, dove through the door of the hooch sprinting for the bunker while everyone else followed. No one had to yell 'INCOMING!'

The first few went over us then we took a few right in our little compound. It was a nice casual pounding that happened once in a while, the rockets were falling in all different areas at a rate of one every fifteen to thirty seconds. There would be the sharp 'CRACK' of an exploding rocket then a little silence so we could crouch in the bunker cringing and wonder if it was over then the scream of another one a little later.

Then one was real close, the ear-splitting crack of the exploding rocket sounded like it was right outside, the flash lit the inside of the bunker for a second! As the shock went away one of the guys peeked out and started to laugh like hell!

'Hey Cohen that was the hooch...its rainin' MPC!'

It really was. Some of it was drifting into the doorway of the bunker. Whoever it was peeked out a little further and gave us the news that it looked like the front of the hooch had taken a direct hit and there was a cloud of MPC floating around out there. Geez...that's where John's locker was.

Before we could start laughing at his misfortune, it took something like four of us to keep him from blindly running outside. There was MPC being found all over the place for days!

Rounds and Powder

Before the beginning of the Tet offensive in '68, we were all called together for a meeting. All of the boat crews attended. We figured that something was up because not only was Smitty there, but so was our commanding officer and some other brass from Da Nang. Like most bad news it began by everyone telling us what a great job we were doing. All we had to do was wait for the 'but' after all of the back patting was over. When it came there was a collective groan from all of us. This was some of the worst news ever.

"Gentlemen," he began, "from now on, due to the logistics situation inland, when carrying artillery loads for the big guns we will be sending everything on the same load. If you have rounds you will also be loaded with an equal amount of powder and fuses for those rounds."

I think everyone's heart sank with that announcement. In the past when we hauled the powder charges for the big guns we were loaded one pallet high in the well deck so that if we were fired on the chances of the powder charges, being hit was minimal. If they were and you had a boat load you wouldn't even know what hit you, it would be over before you could think, one big fast bang. If we were going to be carrying 'everything', we all knew the pallets of powder would be stacked above the top of the well deck, one round and it's all over for everyone on board. A kid with a BB gun could take out one of our boats now...he just had to be a little bit lucky.

The only thing that would change was that we would now play Russian Roulette. Each boat, 'when possible', would only catch one load like this a day, narrowing down our chances as much as they could for the same boat to get hit a few times a day. The other nice change was that the powder charges would no longer be loaded higher than the top of the well deck. We appreciated that.

But, like everything else, 'when possible' wound up being a 'sea story' too. Within about a month we were (each boat) carrying those wonderful loads from one to five trips a day…every day. Pilots have an expression for trips like that; it's called having a high 'pucker-factor'. Then after a while, like so many other things, we became numb to that as well and, just did it.

This chapter was written in the time between 1996 and 2001. Since then, my memory has been improved and more records have become available to the public. I've left most of this the way it was first written, with only a few changes. The rest of it was expanded and re-written last year into what became 'Heart of War'. I did this because many things changed in my life and my eyes were opened to a lot of what I saw then, but – didn't really react to.

Time and knowledge change a lot of things in our lives.

Ferry on the (South) Cua Dai River

This was Dodge City, Indian Territory and Tombstone all rolled into about three square clicks baby, ElephantValley at its best. Up a river 22 miles south of Da Nang, keeping good old Highway 1 open and running with the 860 boat, the bridge had been blown and it (the boat) was the ferry. This was another one of those times when Ms. Fonda's sister (Hanoi Hanna) took great pleasure in reminding us, once in a while, that neither we nor the boat would ever see Da Nang again.

In the year to come this little area would become I-Corps infamous 'Arizona Territory'. Just about as wide open and wild as its namesake

The 860 with the finished bridge in the background. In a matter of weeks the bridge would be gone; wiped out during a flood. Public Domain.

We were surrounded by 'Chuck', cut off most of the time and three things were going on: The SeaBees worked at building/rebuilding the bridge during the day. We...the boat crew...moved as many vehicles as we could across the river in both directions every day, keeping the road open. And the most endearing part of all...

Our buddy 'Chuck' did his best to kill us almost every night. I should also mention that the little bastards had the annoying habit of dropping in the occasional mortar round just to keep us on our toes...the occasional mid-day sniper and floating those damned little mines down the river. 'Charles' was doing his best to be a real little annoying son-of-a-bitch every single chance he had.

And yes, I can write about this a little tongue-in-cheek now, laugh about some of the things that went on there over thirty-five years ago...now. Be assured that while this was going on, not many of us were in a laughing mood about any of it.

There was a platoon of 'India' company of the Third Marine Division on our side of the river. They provided security for our side of the river, us and the road. They had a few recoilless rifles on 'Mules' and one 'Ontos' shotgun that was the main artillery. 'Keloe' company's platoon was a little west in the bush, they sort of roamed around out there and kept Charlie stirred up, at night they dug in and watched our 'front door'.

'Charlie' got even by floating mines down the river every once in a while, hitting the perimeter at night (there had been some real 'mother' firefights) and trying to knock out the watchtower about a mile down the road. Our little brown buddies were also fond of mortar attacks in the middle of the night or any other time they were in the mood.

We had a meeting with the Marines and I got handed over. We would be living on the boat due to security conditions. There had been a few nights that 'Charlie' had tried to sneak down the riverbank and either take it or flank the Marines. We were going to be standing watch every night. If something did happen and the Marines couldn't get down there to help us we were to hold out as long as possible, if worse came to worse we were told to make a run for their compound, first bunker on the left.

Oh...bring the fifty and the ammo; we'd probably need it. We were moving up in the world too. We now had M-14's and all of the bandoliers of strip-clips we wanted. I was impressed.

I had been in Dong Ha shortly before being sent here. My boat was in need of a lot of work so it was being sent to Subic Bay for re-fit and repair. Not just a paint job, after all the hours running (since being delivered) we had two bad engines, the screws were really chewed up and one shaft was bent, the batteries were shot and there were other assorted problems. It was just a work weary worn out boat.

Quint and his crew had taken the boat up there then. After a few weeks, he'd solidified his nickname – 'Quick-draw' – by drawing his 357 Magnum, not clearing the holster and shooting himself in the foot. The round had then, continued through the deck and, right through the top of the port-side fuel tank.

We got our orders in Da Nang, put our gear together and loaded on a truck that would take us through an area called 'Elephant Valley'. We were going south of Da Nang twenty or so miles to where the boat was. The floor of the truck was covered with sandbags and there were Claymore mines (anti-personnel) attached to the outside of the bed. Before we loaded-up we got a little pep talk from our Marines.

Ferry on the (South) Cua Dai River

Yes, I knew 'Elephant Valley' was a hotbed of enemy activity. We didn't have to worry about stampeding elephants though and 'Charlie' was not bashful about hitting anything that traveled the roads through there. Our Marines told us that ambushes were routine and there was always the possibility of mines in the road. Although they didn't think he would go after one truck and a jeep you never really knew, we were armed but also 'cargo' with a job to do once delivered to the boat. Our job was to keep our heads down if anything happened and let them do the fighting; we were only supposed to jump in if it got too hot.

There was a reason for this. The bridge was over a river that cut Highway 1 south of Da Nang, this highway was a vital north south route for our troops. Since the bridge hadn't been built yet, but the An Hoa combat base had been, there was no way to effectively resupply it except by road, the 860 was acting as a ferry until the bridge could be built, someone had to drive the boat and this was one of the times I would hate hearing the word 'experienced'. I was stuck in-country, getting short and was one of the few boat drivers with river experience. We were headed for a place called Hoi An, we were 'breathing', but important cargo riding along with supplies for the boat and the Marines there.

This bass-awkward way of doing things was an earmark of our war.

Once the bridge was finished, it was our job to get the boat back down the river then to Da Nang. For that, we needed a finished bridge and a lot more water in the river.

For the rest of that first day we ran back and forth across the river, bumping on the bottom with the heavier loads. It was late in the year and the river was very low. The only reason we had a channel to run in was because on every trip we were digging it out with our screws. The engineers worked on the bridge, we checked the boat out as we had time and found out that it was about worn out. I figured both screws were pretty chewed up because of the vibration and both shafts were bent to be sure, at anything over about fifteen-hundred RPM the thing would about shake your teeth out!

The ramp was hanging on chains in the down position; there was no reason to raise it anyway. The boat smoked like hell when underway so the 'snipe' figured the injectors were about shot to hell, the compressor still worked pretty well, but slow and the batteries were in good shape. The bilge pump worked and that was a good thing, with the bent shafts both of the shaft packing glands were leaking and couldn't be tightened anymore.

An Ontos – better known as a 'Pig'. Loved the firepower. Source: Public Domain.

The modern day cemetery outside of Phu Loc 6. There are at least 800 graves With dates from 1966 to 1970. Source: Author.

Ferry on the (South) Cua Dai River

Looking toward Phu Loc 6, south end of the bridge. About a week from being finished. Source: Victor Villianois.

A good old 'Mule' with a 90 mm recoilless. Public Domain.

Pre-bridge ferry duty. Public Domain.

I had gone from a boat that was in pretty good condition to one that no one cared about anymore. We did our job while realizing just how bad it could be.

We had a standard PRC field radio, our call-sign was 'Blueberry Pie'. In the morning and afternoon (roughly 12 hours apart) someone from the boat had to contact Da Nang with a situation report, that way they at least knew we were still alive and running.

The bridge wasn't even a fifth of the way across the river at that point.

After our last trip (the highway closed at night for obvious reasons) the company commander met me at the ramp to introduce himself and have a little information session. He was very nice as he explained what areas we should watch at night, we would be pretty much on our own down here, but they wanted us to try and protect the boat if possible and the 'flanking' position where they were pretty much blind.

The river bank was around fifteen feet high and they couldn't see over it, that was our job. We were told that if anything moved out there at night it was fair game "blow it away without any hesitation."

"You can get whatever you need as far as ammo, grenades and that from us; just go see one of the sergeants and they'll fix you up. At night there is no one friendly on the banks or the river...if you see something open up. That little island (he pointed upstream and out in the river) is a place 'Charlie' likes to hide out and harass us from, if you see any fire from there hit 'em with the fifty."

After he left we ate chow (C-Rats, what else), checked weapons and I gave our seaman a quick drill on the fifty...he was green as grass, but a very nice guy. We decided how the watches would be handled and put the boat to bed for the night, I took the first watch. We didn't get much sleep the first night anyway, we were edgy. A couple of hours after dark all hell broke loose down the road at the watchtower! They had a fifty and an M-60 up there, we couldn't see the fire they were taking so it was probably all AK's, what we could see was almost constant tracers from the two machine guns for over an hour. Oh, it would go quiet for a while, but then start up again over and over, there were explosions around the bottom of the tower and out from it.

A little while later there were a couple of mortar rounds dropped close to the compound, a firefight broke out up the river and there were Huey's patrolling around. A couple of the guys walking a loose patrol stopped by to check on us later, they had given a whistle at the top of the road, we talked for a while. They told us not to be bashful about supplies or anything else and "Hey man...screw the boat...it gets too hot down here bug out. Grab some extra ammo, the fifty and haul ass for the first bunker...that's ours." I thanked them and asked how bad it really got.

They told me that this was a typical night...sort of, 'Charlie' had tried to overrun the position a couple of times...not many. "We got 'K' holding the south, but if you see anything coming across the river when it's low like this blow it away and yell for us." They were both short and looking to get out of there, the one guy was on his second tour.

There was a little more noise that night, but it finally calmed down. I got off watch and sort of passed out for a while. This happened almost every night; we got into the habit of napping during the day to store some extra energy. When we didn't have a run across the river, we worked on the boat, played cards or just relaxed. We also took enough time to get to know the guys that were protecting us. The bridge made what I could only describe as agonizingly slow progress across the river; I began to wonder if it would ever get finished.

The one job we really didn't like was taking the 'dead' truck across the river. With all of the fighting going on close around us every three to five days, the Marines would load a truck with the dead enemy. There had been a burial pit dug down off the road to the south just after everyone arrived, for disposing of them. Just moving that truckload of dead across the river wasn't bad enough. They did cover the bodies with lime in the pit, but when the wind changed every once in a while, you got a real strong reminder of death.

I was also introduced to another ritual. Above I mentioned a 'mule' with a ninety millimeter recoilless rifle mounted on it, the 'mule' was just a little four wheeled utility vehicle smaller than a jeep. As I was walking back from the latrine one morning it was parked and a friendly Latino Marine that I knew a little was staring up the river. We talked and I looked the recoilless rifle over, it was one really neat toy.

As we talked about it and I looked it over he kept looking at the same spot, I finally asked him what was going on, there were some people on a low bank of the river about four to five hundred yards away. While we watched, they walked around, squatted, washed, morning 'duties'. He said "That's a free fire zone on K's flank, the 'boss' doesn't want to see shit moving there, I'm waitin' for the crowd to gather."

A few more people joined the little group. He loaded the rifle and pointed to a spot about ten feet away and half way up the barrel saying, "I'm gonna give 'em a little HE (high explosive) this morning, you should stand there." That said, he turned to the compound, cupped his hands to his mouth and yelled, "FIRING!". I had seen a recoilless rifle fire, but never this close. Between the muzzle blast and the back blast it's a different sound, the 'mule' just sort of bounced when it went off and there was an explosion of dust on both ends of it.

The round hit the water well in front of the beach, but didn't explode. We watched it plow through water, the sand and into the foliage beyond before it went off! In seconds the bank was clear. He ejected the shell casing saying "Those dumb shits never learn...I have to do this every few mornings." He was right they just kept coming back.

A few months later the bridge was finished! We were out of a job and would just sit and wait for the river to come back up, this was neat! The engineers had left one span with a hole big enough for us to squeeze through...just, for the first day it was open we just sat around and relaxed. We got the boat ready to leave and I checked the fuel tanks, I figured we had more than enough fuel to make it back to Da Nang, the only problem was that we needed a lot more water in the river, about four more feet. Someone had come up from Da Nang with an old map of the river; we were supposed to get the Marines to call ops there before we left. I would then make my last situation report call and haul ass. He became known as 'Ensign Benson', he was a young ensign about a year older than I was and fresh out of the academy then fresh in country. God was he green! I had more time on the latrine than he had in Nam!

And...he was trapped, that afternoon they closed the highway.

As the afternoon wore on we also found out that he was scared to death and bordering on being an idiot. I mean, we were all scared, but there was no reason to go over the edge, as evening approached we began our usual weapons check and got ready for whatever would happen. Benson hid.

A little before dusk, a couple of the Marines walked down to check on us and give us the 'skinny' that 'Charles' was going to try overrun the compound that night. 'K' was spread out to the west, but if he got past them we were probably going to be 'in the shit', they told us that there were a few gunships on call and 'arty' (artillery) had the area 'dialed in'. I did not want to hear that, I was finally starting to get 'short' myself.

The one Marine said, "Look man, same old shit. They flank us if they get by you guys…we're asking you to hold it if you can. Same deal, it gets too bad run for the bunker, but bring the fifty…if not put a 'ham and eggs' (frag grenade) in the breach before you bug out." We traded 'good-lucks' and they walked back up to the compound, we were so close to getting out of here…damn.

Ensign Benson was not a happy camper.

This was one night that I got everyone in the safety of the well deck, that put almost half an inch of steel between us and 'Charles'. As darkness fell I double checked the fifty and we moved all of the weapons and ammo down there with us, to this point I had never fired a fifty in anger, but had been through weapons school in Pendleton. I did know how to use it. Scared yes, but what else do you do? I had also made peace with myself months ago, I was pretty sure I could kill someone or at least defend the boat.

Ferry on the (South) Cua Dai River

We had everything we needed, about three thousand rounds for the fifty, extra mags for the M-14's, taped together in 2's and lots of 'strip clips' to re-load the mags, almost a full case of frag grenades and a lot of pop flares. My snipe was motivated, he now had his M-2 carbine and my M-14.

I would man the fifty, I made sure that the seaman (who just became my loader/feeder) knew what to do and how to do it. We also put together some longer belts of ammo to cut down on fumbling around for it in the dark. Yes kiddies...I know...short controlled bursts, we didn't have a spare barrel that time. Besides, the last thing you want to do is change-out the barrel of a fifty...in the dark...under extreme pressure.

About an hour later 'K' company took on 'Charlie' and the watchtower was hit very hard. Our entire area became illuminated by one flare after another! I kept the fifty pointed right down the center of the river bank while we took turns with the field glasses scanning the area behind the boat on the other bank upriver and up the bank in front of us. 'K' company was in a fight for its life!

Even from where we were, it was more than evident that they were getting hit harder than ever before, out in the bush not more than three hundred yards away there were flares hanging in the air. Under the flares there were constant explosions all over the place. Tracers bounced in all directions as a huge firefight went on and on. After a while we concentrated hard very on the riverbank in front of us if anything moved there or on the river behind us it was going to be blown away. In my mind I knew we were holding the left flank for the company of Marines that were our security, I committed myself to try and defend it even though I was scared shitless like the rest.

Yep, 'John Wayne' (me) was just as scared as everyone else.

When there weren't any flares the night was pitch black, when there was no firing it was dead calm, not even a little puff of air. We were sweating in our gear like everyone else, hearts pounding and dry mouthed while we waited. When all of the flares stopped burning I swore I saw things moving out there, it was just my mind playing tricks. When the flares were illuminating the area with their eerie pink back and forth light I was positive things were moving around out there!

Suddenly there was firing from the compound across the area directly in front of them, flares popped upward into the sky and lit up the night, I strained like hell to see as far as possible down the riverbank. The watchtower down the road was under attack again and there was a Huey in the area, Ensign Benson was hunkered down in a corner of the well deck. This was one hell of a night.

Things sort of died down after a while except from the area where 'K' company was, there was still sporadic fire there and a few explosions once in a while, flares were still shooting up all over.

The Huey made a pass on the other side of the river then headed up the river going pretty slow, as they approached the little island there was a stream of tracers sent in its direction, they were white tracers so it was the enemy. I won't ever know if the chopper took any hits, but I'm sure that 'Charles' was sorry he did what he did.

This was one of the ones with mini-guns and a nose load of M-79 grenades, we watched as the mini-guns pounded the area that the fire had come from then they unloaded the M-79's on the same area. Not only was it pretty impressive, but there was no more fire from that area, they were either dead or out cold after that.

'K' company continued to have contact on and off until just before dawn, a few times one of the guys from the bunker came down to check on us, I mean we were the ones that were supposed to hold the left flank. During whispered conversation I found out that 'K' was getting its ass kicked, but had held the position and kept 'Charlie' from getting through. We shared some smokes and I noticed he was shaking too, I didn't feel so bad just then.

The next morning, we found out that 'K' had taken over eighty percent casualties, but held the position and turned 'Charlie' back.

I have nothing but absolute admiration for Marines to this day.

The bridge over the South Dai was all wood, the next afternoon about one PM our buddy 'Charles' put a WP round in it a little over half way to the other side. Wood soaked with creosote makes one hell of a fire when lit properly, the one WP round did it just right. After all of the months of work the new bridge was burning like a gasoline soaked Kotex!

Ohhhhhhhh shit! We weren't going anywhere for a while now. Damn!

I'm getting 'short'. Benson has grabbed all of the good C-Rats and was now moving into after steering. The road is closed and the brass in Da Nang have forgotten about him…just what I needed!

The Marine engineers and the Marines were running all over the place and trying to figure out how to put the fire out, we can't just call the local fire department and have them do it, there were no pumps or anything to put water on it. That one WP round did a good job. Trying to think about how to help I remembered the satchel charge I have to destroy the boat in an emergency, blowing this on the bridge deck may either blow the fire out or blow it (the bridge) apart enough to save this end of it.

I ran up to the road to chase a Marine down on the bridge, we talk and I explain what I have in mind. He agrees and tells me to get the satchel charge.

In a few minutes I'm running back across the bridge with the charge in hand and the 'trigger' out to pass it off to him, he takes it pulls the pin on the trigger and slides it across the deck of the bridge...we both duck and run. Twenty seconds later there is one hell of an explosion as all four sticks of C-4 go off, otherwise nothing changes much. Material from the bridge flies all over the place, but the other end of the bridge continues to burn, the fire on our side dies and goes out.

Ensign Benson has really pissed someone off in Da Nang, he is told to stay with the boat, and even though the road is open again we are stuck with him. He has set up his home in after steering and only comes out to take a dump once in a while, as an officer he uses his rank to take the best of the C-Rats. The engineers go back to work on the bridge and we are now operating as the ferry again. Since we are stuck here a tanker is sent to top off our tanks while the bridge is rebuilt...again.

I am getting shorter as we speak and really interested in getting back to Da Nang before I get my sorry ass killed, there is no relief and 'Benson' spends the next month living in the after steering space and waiting.

One day about a month later, 'Benson' is ordered to return with the supply truck and the bridge is just about finished...again, we moved the boat to the lower side of the bridge and hoped the water would come up a little so that we can leave the hell out of there. We sit and wait and kill time, but can't go anywhere until we have at least one good storm to bring the river level up a little, we spend our days tied up to the lower side of the bridge bow first, waiting, playing cards and bored to tears.

We also get some strange looks from the passing traffic on the bridge. Big boat, almost no water in the river, their expressions are sort of, 'How the hell did that get here?"

Charles does his job almost every night, but doesn't get lucky with the bridge again, we have permission to head for Da Nang as soon as there are a few more feet of water in the river, all of us are wishing for a little bit of rain. We did take this leisure time to get to know the Marines a little better. Like us, they are tired, bored and sick of being stuck here for so long. They were really hoping to get relieved soon.

The only reason that they are still there is because of three sailors and a riverboat. They can't leave until we leave...period.

But then again, sometimes, you don't really want what you wish for.

It began to rain where we were, but up in the mountains it was pouring! Around six hours later the river began to rise, but just a little. Around evening we did notice an increase, but nothing to worry about, the next morning we would probably be on our way back down the river and on to Da Nang for a little rest and enjoyment.

That night we went to visit the Marines for what we thought would be the last time. We ate dinner with them and said goodbye all around before returning to the boat. Before nightfall I broke out the map I had and we stowed our gear below, we were on our way home, the river had come up some more and by morning it would be adios bridge!

In my dreams.

For some reason, I sacked out in the soaking wet con while the guys went below. I'll never know why. I was curled up in a few blankets and dripping wet, but sleeping soundly when something woke me up. Over the thunder and the din of the drumming rain, debris in the river banging off the boat, the crashing sound of the bridge splintering apart woke me up.

To this day I can remember what it looked like when I stood up in the con, the rain was pouring down like hell and it was pitch black, but I could see the bridge through it. Looking to my left I could clearly see the bridge leaning downriver, there was the sound of cracking breaking timber even above the rain and the sound of the river.

When we sacked out we were only about five feet up the pilings that were almost twenty feet tall on this end of the bridge, now we were almost level with the road deck of the bridge! The rain was pouring down and the river sounded like it was ripping by the boat! I could see what was happening because the Marines were popping a flare once in a while to keep an eye on the bridge and us, they had seen debris beginning to build up against it and were just about to come see if we were awake or even knew what was happening.

As I began to come to my senses I watched as the main bridge span began folding downriver, I was watching it as if in slow motion while it collapsed and disappeared in the swiftly moving river lit by the flickering pale pink light of the flares.

Ferry on the (South) Cua Dai River

Alone in the con in the middle of the night, we will be tied up to what remains of the bridge in a minute and wearing it, blind and disoriented we will have to go somewhere or just try to hang on (where?) until the wet dawn breaks…

In desperation I realize that I'm about to hold reveille on two guys sleeping peacefully in the nice dry engine room below me. I only thank my lucky stars that I was stupid enough to try to sleep in the wet con. As swift and high as the river was we could have greeted the morning with the surprise of being hung up downriver lost or worse…floating in the South China Sea still tied up to what remained of the bridge.

It's a boat with almost fifteen-hundred horsepower and a lot of push…in desperation I push the engine controls forward and push the buttons for the air starters…if the starters roll them through to get one cylinder to fire both banks will light as the transmissions pull the second engine in…oh the love of diesels.

And automatic transmissions.

The air starters made their high pitched scream and roll the engines, two light, there is a little drag on these two as the transmissions try to roll the remaining engine in on each bank…they light! As the exhaust note rises some I push both throttles full ahead and hold them there, the engines respond and the boat begins to rattle like hell as the revs go up past two thousand RPM topping out at around twenty five hundred and pushing like hell!

The snipe and the seaman pop up from the engine room into the pouring rain to stand in front of the con and look around, suddenly they realize what is going on and are amazed...soaking wet and amazed!

As most of the bridge collapses into the river in pieces, we are sitting there at 'all ahead fantastic' holding the last hundred feet of the bridge in place. Hold it up or wear it. If the shafts weren't bent and the screws not chewed to shit we could be turning about three thousand revs...instead my tachs are flipping between twenty-two hundred and twenty-eight hundred RPM, the boat is rattling like hell, but holding the bridge...just.

We sit there and push while the boat tries to shake apart, while we do the engines that have only been a little above idle for the past six months blow the carbon out and take on the old throaty roar of an eight boat, ratting our teeth out, but running well...the Marines keep popping flares.

Over the roar of the exhaust the noise from the engine room the drumming rain and the pounding of the boat I yell 'HEY!' to my snipe and seaman, they turn to look at me as I toss two wet ponchos over the con to them.

Smiling in the dim light of the flares they shake them out and put them on.

My snipe remembers that the packing glands are simply pouring water into the boat now and disappears below to start the bilge pump...we push against the bridge for the next few hours until the wet slate gray dawn begins to break.

The rain slows to a drizzle, then stops. We are now almost level with the deck of the bridge and we have been rattled for almost three hours, the river is raging and there is a lot of stuff coming down. For the past hours it has bounced off of our bow and been dinged by the screws, trees, houses and anything else in the river.

A couple of Marines walk out onto the bridge and look then wave, we wave back while having coffee and eating some cold C-Rats, the river is still moving fast and we remain at full throttle...shaking our guts out.

They look around and shrug, we shrug back, we are still just holding the boat if we would cast off we would get pushed down the river by the current.

We exchange a 'thumbs-up' and they are gone.

A few hours later the river begins to go down a little, but not as fast as it rose, when I think it's slowed down enough that we can make some way upstream we ease our lines then untie from the remains of the bridge and head for the compound, we can now drive right up to the commander's bunker! The river had risen almost sixteen feet in under twelve hours, we can't tell where the river 'was' now and everything is flooded as far as we can see. There are only little 'islands' of high ground sticking up all around and trees.

Our first job is to go look for stranded Marines then bring them back to what we have left of 'high-ground', that is mostly a strip of raised road. We do that as well as move a few vehicles across the river as the ferry. That job (of gathering stranded Marines) was finished within a few hours. As the water begins to recede we find ourselves beaching farther and farther from the road.

Waiting for us (at the end of one trip) is a lieutenant and a platoon of Marines. I pull in and put the ramp close to him, he boards and walks right up to the con to lean over "We need to go huntin' us some 'gooks'...let me load my boys and we'll go upriver for a while."

That wasn't a question, it was an order, in five minutes we had a reinforced platoon aboard and were headed upriver. For the next few hours we roamed everywhere I thought I could put the boat and we looked for anyone that was moving.

They have two M-60 machine guns, grenade launchers and a 'rocket' (bazooka), plus the riflemen. We have the fifty and a lot of ammo. The Marines are clearly on a mission, they want to kick some ass and vent a lot of frustration while being very mobile. Under a low hanging gray overcast sky we cruise around, the lieutenant rides in the con with me and looks for targets, when something is spotted it's destroyed.

When we did finally turn around and head for the compound there had to be over twenty (enemy) bodies floating in the river.

We dropped our platoon off and spent the next few hours 'fetching' more stranded Marines from all over and taking them back to high ground. I had been keeping an eye on the river as it went down and adjusting my landing points because I didn't want to be too far out of the river and strand the boat with a mistake that could put us out of action. I did know a lot of the topography around the river and that even (if I started) bumping along the bottom I knew the boat could dig itself out. This all changed on my final and almost disastrous trip to the raised roadway near the Marine camp.

We had just brought a tank across the river and I had to have him put it all the way in the back of the well deck to make the landing point, the boat had grounded out in a new area and the river was going down a lot faster now. Being a little limited in my options to get back close to the river I tried to choose the best route and do it fast, luck wasn't with me that day. As I backed down dragging the boat over the bottom and trying to wiggle it a little to force water under the boat we all heard a sickening 'thump' as the left bank ran away, we had lost the screw on that bank! On all of the boats I had ever been on we had never once tossed a screw...damn!

I shut that bank down and put the other one in neutral to check things out, even if we could find the screw there was no way we were going to find the nut to hold it on, or the key. Our only choice was to continue to try and drag the boat with just one screw. The Marines realized we were in trouble and we started to shout back and forth, it was still too deep to use a tank to help us with a push or anything, the only thing I could think of was to have some 'bodies' walk the area around the boat and try and find deeper water. I put my seaman in the water and a few Marines jumped in to help, the water was chest deep as they slogged out to us and went behind the boat.

With this group walking back and forth they found an area that was a little deeper, I eased the boat into it and suddenly wasn't on the bottom anymore! They swam around to the ramp and boarded the boat for a ride back to shore where we were met by the Marine officer in charge, in a short pow-wow I explained what the problem was and, what we needed. Yes, I could still operate as the ferry, but would have to be very careful; with only one screw an 8-boat was pretty underpowered.

As we went back to work I made the call to Da Nang, in an hour we were informed that not only did we have a new screw and the other parts on the way, but we were also getting two divers to put it back on...the next day. That was very good news because we had been trying to figure out how we were going to do it ourselves! I had figured that all the 'chewing' on the bottom of the river had sheared the big shaft key off, once the screw could spin on the shaft it had probably backed the nut off after shearing the cotter pin.

We were right, when the divers showed up the next day it took hours to get the screw back on, the one problem was that they had to everything by feel down there. Even on a bright sunny day they had no visibility down there, they had to do everything by touch, just finding the sheared key in the keyway and replacing it took about an hour. While they worked away traffic backed up on both sides of the river, around noon we had our new bronze installed (which probably cost around a thousand dollars or more) and were back under way. Working, but not going anywhere downriver for a while, once again the SeaBees went back to work rebuilding that damned bridge.

I don't remember who my replacement was, but a few weeks later I was recalled to Da Nang, I had thirty days of leave coming in the 'world'. This would be a round trip for me; I was coming back for another tour.

I must have been pretty numb by then too. I have no memory of getting my gear together or the truck ride back up Highway 1 to Da Nang. The next thing I remember is getting aboard the APL and really longing for a hot shower and some bad Navy chow.

Postscript

As I worked on this I was also posting to many guest books on Brown Water Navy web sites. I have done this for years and never had a response from anyone who served on the boats up north. Not even anyone that served in Da Nang in the early years, I was beginning to think that I would never make contact with anyone else that served during that time.

Ferry on the (South) Cua Dai River

I realized that we had been a small group (the ones of us on ops), but even out of a hundred guys a few had to be online.

After a while I began to think I would never make contact with anyone, those three years of my life were just a bad dream that there was no waking from.

One day I opened a piece of email from someone I didn't recognize, I opened it because the address (ahead of my email address) read 'lcm8 danang' and the subject line read 'response'. The next one that proved that it wasn't a bad dream contained the words 'blueberry pie'. Reading the old call sign of that boat sent a shock through me like a bolt of lightning; I had forgotten that part of it after all of the years.

As the months wore on, we stayed in constant touch, each refreshing the other's memory about different things that happened during our first tour. He went to the fleet and I spent two more tours on the rivers, thanks to becoming what was called 'vital personnel'.

A Word About the Pictures

Since all of mine were lost just prior to my return to the States, I've had to rely on the understanding and great generosity of others who served in the same areas. Since beggars can't be choosers and (most of us didn't realize how important they might be in the far future), like our memories, many of them have faded a little. Also, some of the maps and other items found on the web may be very general in nature. This couldn't be helped.

I have tried to give full and complete credit for all of the donated items and only used those when I was given permission to do so.

<u>One very important note:</u>

The picture is of Ken Brown and was taken just before his death. If anyone knows how to get in touch with any of his family please contact me. I would love to get this picture back to them before it gets lost.

End of whining.

Tan My/Hue and the Perfume River

By the time I was transferred (via the 860 and a round trip to the 'world') to Tan My things on the Perfume River were well under way, there had been a base camp established on a peninsula near the mouth of the river. We had a nice camp area that had been built by the Sea Bees and the Marines, we had nice hooches bunkers were still eating C-Rats (once in a while), but also had something to die for...an EM club! We had power via a generator, an actual boat repair shop (run by 'Frosty' Cain) and were living pretty nice for a change, it was also pretty peaceful in this area...for now.

One of the reasons for the peace was the amount of Marines in our area, there was an Amtrak battalion and a few companies of Marines to keep 'Charlie' on the run most of the time. Our duty was pretty easy while I was in that area, there was enough time to enjoy the comfort of hot showers, good bunks and the EM club. Life was good.

As I remember there were four of us running 8-Boats at any one time, there were also a few assorted 6-Boats with us, some a regular Mike-6 and a few were rebuilt as 'pusher-boats'. I don't remember what my boat number was there, but I had a pretty good crew and the boat was in good shape. We also had 'Frosty' and his gang in the repair shack which was a blessing, not just for us, but the Marines. I found out in short order that these guys really could do anything with nothing, they were first class 'comshaw' artists led by 'Mr. Comshaw' himself 'Frosty', if they couldn't misappropriate what we needed they would steal it, if all else failed they made it from scratch.

The Marines across the channel loved 'Frosty', you see he was a master welder and fabricator, since all of their vehicles were steel and saw a lot of service there were times the kid came in real handy to help them out. With either a stick welder or gas he was an artist with steel and rods, he was also someone that could actually 'see' what needed to be done to solve the problem and simply got it done...no problem.

Our jobs were fairly easy and when compared to Cua Viet sometimes downright boring, we actually had some time off (to enjoy the club) and were in a secure situation. Most of the time we took turns running as a ferry between our side and the Marine base until we got a section of a pontoon bridge with an engine and propeller mounted on each end, which became the official ferry.

We hauled a lot of cargo from ships seaside upriver to the ramp at Hue City, I remember a lot of days that we hauled 'reefers' of frozen food in an endless line. These 'reefers' were a smaller version of today's shipping container and called (then) a 'conex-box', we gave them express service up the river. After all we were running that river with LCU/YFU's and we could run circles around them even loaded, I did that one day just for the hell of it and yes, I got my ass chewed out for the stunt. Hell, we were the fastest thing on that river then and ran it wide open, every trip.

The LCU (I buzzed) had left the ramp at Hue City as we were hitting the beach, we were unloaded in half an hour and on our way back out for another load, there was a nice long stretch of river almost two miles long after leaving the ramp, it was a beautiful part of the river lined with trees on both sides and fairly wide, we caught the LCU at the end of this stretch.

He was running like a snail with a broken leg-thing. We were going 'all-ahead-fantastic' and caught him easily. I came up on his right side checking to make sure there was no other traffic on the river. Clearing his bow by fifty or so feet I kicked the helm over to the left and crossed him, clearing him again I held the helm over until I could put the boat on course back upriver. We had every ones attention on board the LCU...especially the CPO that was the skipper of the boat.

I made the same turn behind the boat as my crew hung on then squared it up and ran past it leaving them behind us, there was a lot of finger waving and yelling from both crews as we outran them. Okay, we weighed about fifty and one hundred fifty tons respectively and we were in motion when I did it. The little 'show-boat' stunt just pissed off the CO of the slow LCU and he called base.

That stunt got me a good natured ass chewing from our NCO in charge, at the end of it he just asked me to not to 'buzz' any more U-boats, I sort of, agreed not to.

Our other duty while in Tan My was to haul barges up and down the river and that was a real thrill in a way! The one-hundred foot long barges were loaded with crushed stone from a quarry down south of us somewhere. It was being used as a road base for Highway 1. An ocean going tugboat would bring three or four of these to within something like a mile of the river entrance. It was our job to get the barges from him (exchanging empties for full ones) then put them in a little backwater area before we took them upriver.

Even with two boats making the exchange of the barges it was an all day job for us. We could move the empties around pretty easily, the loaded ones probably outweighed us something like eight to one. But, just like a tow boat on the Mississippi, we handled them slow and easy. It took forever to get them going and a long time to stop them, every bend going upriver had to be thought about way in advance and planned.

The loaded ones were actually easier because you could make up the 'tow' from the stern (rear) of the barge and see over the cargo of stone. Empty they were a few feet taller than an 8-boat and our ramp would ride under them; unloaded barges were moved from the side with us tied up near the rear. From my position in the con I was blind on that side as soon as we tied up, you trusted your seaman to ride on the barge and give directions to avoid other traffic.

My guys were always better than 'pretty good' at this job. The only times I remember having a problem was second guessing them or hitting a shallow spot with a loaded one on the way up. Those sudden stops could really hurt, after a few trips we all learned to hang onto something just in case I was a little out of position in the channel.

The nice part about it was that barge handling was like having a day off. You ate chow in the morning then got your crew together for the run out to the holding area. By the time you made up the first tow it was nine-o'clock or later, it took a minimum of three hours to get it to the ramp at Hue City. A nice slow easy trip with only a few of us paying attention at any one time, everyone else relaxed.

The trip down with an empty was faster, but by the time you took the second one up it was time for chow and a few beer calls at the club. If there were four barges the next day was just as easy, the hardest part of the trip was making (tying) up to the tow.

We Get 'Monitors' for a Few Months.

Just after Christmas in 1967 I returned from thirty day leave to once again find myself up a river, the same old Cua Viet I'd left what seemed like hours before. During my short time away there had been a lot of changes and none of them were any good. Upon my arrival in Da Nang I was assigned a boat and a new crew and we were sent back up north.

The 'monitors' were converted Mike (LCM) 6 boats, a smaller and slower landing craft, left over from World War II. The idea was to load them with guns, beef-up the armor and use them for not only mine sweepers but, daylight river patrol. There had been some success using them in the Mekong Delta – we had two sent up to help us – an 'Alpha' and a 'Tango'. The Alpha was the command and control boat, the Tango was the armed/heavily armored minesweeper. The Tango – and most of the crew – would become a 'sacrifice' within two months. There were 'nuisance' mines in the delta; we had – on the Cua Viet – the real thing...five hundred to seven hundred and fifty pound bombs...delivered to the DMZ by us; the duds put to use by Chuck.

The sweep boats dragged a grappling hook, at the end of about one hundred feet of cable. The idea was to snag the wires and make detonation (from shore) useless by pulling the wires into the river. The problem was that the sweep boats were ahead of the grapple.

We Get 'Monitors' for a Few Months

I was not prepared for what I would find nor just how bad it would become in the next few months as we (once again) followed a convoy of LCU's up the coast and into the Cua Viet River. There was always the threat of floating mines as well as the re-wired bombs that the enemy put into the river with the intention of blowing up one of our boats.

He had finally scored his first hit. Charlie White's boat had taken a direct hit by a 'bomb' mine. He, his engineman, seaman and another crewmember had all died in it. The boat laid upside down just outside of the river channel, I was told that none of the bodies had been recovered and that (from an eyewitness) the engines and transmissions had been blown up out of the boat.

There were now two monitors stationed there to assist our mine sweeper as well as provide convoy security for us. The canopy over our con was ordered removed right away as a precaution to not get caught under it. The space of shade it had provided in the blazing sunlight was now gone. The rest of the bad news was that the enemy had started to increase his activity along the river. There had been sporadic harassment in the past. Now, for the past month, this had increased dramatically as Tet approached. The word was that the enemy wanted to sink one or more boats (in the channel) to close the river and put us out of business for the Tet Offensive. The increase of automatic weapons fire larger than the AK-47 was up and now they were also using more RPG's, mortars and occasional small recoilless rifles on us. Even with the Marines patrolling the river banks as much as possible the enemy could still get past or through them to set up long enough to hit us then slip quickly away.

A few of the crews had built what we referred to as 'flower boxes' outboard of the con area as protection for the crew in the con. The idea was to absorb the explosion of an RPG before it got to the quarter inch steel which was no protection from them. These were wooden boxes filled with sand and they did work.

Before I'd gone on leave, we had been going upriver behind the LCM-6 that was our mine sweeper, in convoy for the first trip of the day. Now it as well as the one monitor were both dragging grappling hooks trying to snare the wires which were used to trigger the mines. It only took old 'Chuck' a little time before he started putting a few mines in the part of the channel they (our minesweepers) ran in close, to the shore. The first trip of the day, in convoy and going very slow, was not something any of us looked forward to, not one little bit.

The Mike-6 and the monitor were slow to begin with, cruising even slower in the morning to carefully drag the sweep-gear. Our speed was something like a brisk trot/jog so that first twelve mile trip to Dong Ha seemed endlessly agonizing and far longer than necessary, but it was. I will guarantee you that everyone in that first trip was wide awake, on-point and puckered up good and tight for the entire duration of it.

There was, however, some good news.

All we had to worry/think about were the command detonated mines, the floating mines, direct and in-direct mortar/recoilless rifle fire, light and heavy small arms and machine gun fire from the riverbanks and...maybe, breaking down. The good news was that we didn't have to worry about being attacked from the air!

I should probably also explain that not only were these command detonated 'mines' re-cycled ordinance, but our own stuff being used against us. That had to be the most cutting irony of this entire mess.

We Get 'Monitors' for a Few Months

The DMZ was only 3.5 miles away and the Air Force used B-52's to drop tons of bombs there almost every night. The thought was that the enemy was moving through there on his way south, the night time bombing would disrupt his activity. It would have, but after 'Chuck' caught on to this he simply started moving into Laos then south.

I have no idea what the ratio of good bombs to duds was, but it was good enough for the enemy. They would move through the DMZ collect some dud 250 and 500 pound bombs, re-wire the fuses then either bury them in a road or in our case dump them in the river channel.

They only needed enough light wire (like telephone wire) to reach back to the river bank so they could hide in the tall grass and wait for a boat to come by, a D-cell flashlight or a lantern battery provided the power to fire the fuse.

If someone on the crew was alert enough you might also see the 'float' they used on the wire, this helped line up the bomb with the boat for a better shot at you.

However, after that first 'white-knuckle' trip, we were free to run the river as fast as we could...and we did! For the rest of the day the monitors and our one PBR did patrol duty all up and down the river trying to get 'Charlie' to come out and play. Sometimes he did, sometimes he didn't.

The enemy's biggest thrill had to be the morning that he destroyed the one monitor. It was a beautiful morning, hardly a cloud in the brilliant blue sky, the breeze blowing in from the South China Sea was so light that the air around us seemed calm as we went upriver.

When the (bomb) mine went off under the boat we felt the hard concussion at about the same time that the monitor was blown into the air above a huge fountain of water! Both shocked and sad we all watched as it turned over in the air while pieces flew off in all directions.

The only survivors were a seaman and the officer in charge, both had been above decks working the mine sweeping gear. Badly wounded, but alive.

 In the next few days, the other monitor returned to the safer waters of the Mekong Delta. Down there they had smaller mines to worry about.

'Granny' Flag Wipes Out our Favorite Bar

This incident happened a little over halfway through my first tour. NSA Da Nang hadn't gone beyond cargo operations in the Da Nang area. I was crewing for old Horace D. At this time the city of Da Nang was still open to us and when not on duty we could roam pretty much at will, there was a PX outside of the city and it was easy to bum a ride there.

A very old picture of the original Bamboo Bar. Picture Donated by 'Tam'.

We knew the town well enough to stay out of the bad areas. We had our favorite bars and restaurants, we were at this time still being paid in and carrying American 'greenbacks' which the Vietnamese loved to take. This continued for a few more months until the conversion was made to MPC or Military Payment Certificates, we called it funny money or Monopoly money, the locals didn't like taking it because they had no way to convert it.

At least until the black market really got going.

We also had our own 'racket' going on the side as I mentioned before, since we hauled lots of cargo (which included things going to the local PX) we had a lot of overflow stashed away on the boats most of the time. If you wanted to go to town and drink till curfew for nothing you simply took a carton of fresh American cigarettes with you gave them to the mama-san that owned the bar and sat back to enjoy the night.

Slip her something like the cigarettes, a Japanese transistor radio and a handful of batteries and you not only got her undying affection, but drank, got a room if you wanted one and a choice of a girl. Mama-sans didn't give 'rain checks' so you either did it that night or brought more back when you had time to spend it.

One of our favorite places to hang out was called the Bamboo Bar. This nice little joint was almost directly across the river from Camp Tien Sha. It wasn't real big inside, but it had a covered veranda that ran around three sides. There were tables out there, they served pretty good native food and the beer and booze was reasonably priced. The owners and staff were all very friendly. Sure they were; we spent a lot of money there and it was all green.

On the veranda of the Bamboo Bar; probably in late 1968. Looking way too serious.

Like I said it was directly across the river from Tien Sha, rather than making the trip way upriver to the bridge the brass had started to use one of the 8-boats as a ferry. It ran pretty much from dawn to dusk and cut something like six miles off of the trip from the camp to downtown, everyone took turns crewing it because it was one real boring job.

The landing on the Da Nang side was right beside this bar, I shouldn't have to tell the rest of the story...but I will. Besides, the one picture of me was taken one afternoon while on the veranda of the 'late' bar to be.

At this point we had boats and crews, but not the mass of cargo to haul yet, some of us were still living in Camp Tien Sha and had free time. On this afternoon a bunch of us went to town and then to the Bamboo Bar for food and drink, okay mostly drink, 'Granny' Flagg was running the ferry that afternoon and it was a moderately hot day.

'Granny' Flag Wipes Out our Favorite Bar

We sort of took over the bar then moved out onto the veranda where it was cooler after a while to talk and have some drinks; this was probably about the time we had become used to the stench of Vietnam too.

Flagg made a few trips back and forth. We were watching him run the boat in his usual casual professional manner and mostly checking on who was coming and going, there could be guys that we knew and we would invite them to join our little party. We also watched ole' Granny because he was one of the 'old salts' in the unit; a real character and a nice guy all around, we both respected and looked up to him and a few others. Besides, most of the older guys were more than a little 'colorful' in their own ways.

On one trip he unloaded his passengers and since there wasn't anyone on either side of the river he sat there for a while waiting, the engines idling ahead just enough to keep the boat pushing against the ramp. Since we had known each other for a while eventually we said hello, he also knew that I was studying for my E-4 exam and that I was going for boatswains mate third class. He and a few of the other boat drivers had started to refer to me as 'Boats' which is the common term for addressing someone of that job description in the Navy. He left the con walked over to the handrail and shouted up 'Hey 'Boats' throw me down a beer...I'll pay 'ya later.'

Nineteen and easily led I got one of the big bottles of '33' beer and passed it down to him, like I said he was one of our heroes anyway.

We all drank the Vietnamese beer and it was pretty wicked stuff, if I remember the alcohol level in it was about thirty-three percent, if you compared it to the beer we got at the base club it was like comparing diesel fuel to rocket fuel. Most of us didn't drink whiskey because it was watered down and you could get a much better buzz going on the beer.

Flagg popped the bottle and I guess he must have been pretty dry, within two trips he was ready to toss it back up in exchange for a full one, nice guy that I was I helped him out. Now Flagg was a little skinny guy that stood about five feet seven inches and he had just put away thirty ounces of 'real' beer in under half an hour. He was about to repeat it, yep I said thirty ounces these were no 'pony' bottles of Miller Light.

On his next trip over, everyone (on his crew) was sort of hanging on pretty hard except for his human cargo. He came in a little too fast and when he hit the riverbank/ramp the jeep he was hauling skidded about three feet forward. If the driver wouldn't have had his foot on the brake, the jeep would have simply unloaded itself.

Like most of us seamen, Flagg's was riding back and forth on the forward 'butt'. A 'butt' was used to tie the boat up, it was a six inch steel tube welded upright on the deck with about an eight inch diameter flat top and one inch round steel bars facing fore and aft. You sat down on it and just rode there; this kid was hanging on tight and still almost got launched over the bow when the boat came to a sudden stop. He looked up at us and just rolled his eyes before walking the gunwale (carefully) back to the con area, he knew it was a lot safer there!

There were more trips and more beers passed down as the sun set over Da Nang, our party was going pretty well and so was the one on the boat.

By the time Flagg needed something like his fourth beer, it was obvious to everyone except him that he was getting pretty 'cranked'. It was dark, the lights in the bar were on and we were having a pretty good party. Flagg was having a problem finding either side of the river with much accuracy and there had been a near miss of the poles holding up the bar.

Right poles, most of this bar hung out over the river, if I remember right something like sixty percent of it was sitting on wooden poles sunk in the river bank and river for support. Where we were on the veranda it was around fifteen feet above the river.

When leaving our side he had been backing clear of the bar before swinging the boat around…had been. On the last few trips not only had he come close to hitting the poles on the way in, but wasn't compensating for the current on the way out, the bow had been a little close as he began to swing the boat.

We all thought it was pretty funny.

Someone suggested it was about time to leave before we would have to catch a truck and ride all the way around. It was getting late; the boat had been sitting there, but was now loading a truck for Tien Sha. We made it out of the bar, but didn't get to the ramp in time to catch him.

This was a good thing. He backed away and started swinging the boat a little too soon. We got to watch from the safety of the ramp as fifty tons of Mike-8 went through those poles like matchsticks, with the ramp of the boat down the bar never had a chance. That five or so tons of steel ramp being swung by the moving boat went through those poles like an axe. With part of the support gone the rest couldn't hold the bar up. We watched as our favorite joint broke apart and came crashing down on the river bank and into the river, veranda first then the rest of it just sort of settled in the direction of the river before following the veranda into a heap of rubble as the people inside yelled, screamed and ran! Flagg was on his way to the other side of the river, probably the only one oblivious to the total destruction he had just caused. Party over folks!

My group caught a truck for the long ride back to camp.

I never did find out what happened to Flagg.

Ken Menke and Khe Sanh

One day in '04 or '05, I got a wild hair and tried to contact a guy called Ken Menke. Ken was a high school friend; he was what I'd classify as a good but casual friend – he was more academic, in band and other things, I was more just a general student. He lived in a very small village that straddled old Route 28 about five miles from our farm. Other than school, Ken was a pretty laid-back guy who didn't really get into anything too deep or intense. There was a time, in the summer of '64 that we lost contact for a while. After that I went to basic and lost contact with everyone I'd known in school. Everyone I'd known in life, other than my family.

One day, for some unknown reason, I just decided that I should try and find him. After all of those years just give him a call, see how he was doing and how his life was. I don't know why I waited so long – other than just being totally screwed-up - because, I never expected to hear what I was about to hear.

The best date I can put on this is (about) April 1968. It was at the end of the siege, when the main body of the Marines moved out and, turned it over to the Army.

I've mentioned, more than once, that there were times that we were just plain worn out, worn down. There was no rotation, to the rear, for even a few days of R&R. Everything just soaked into you – all the way to the bone – and set up camp there. Once there, it gnawed at you, every waking moment of every day. We didn't know what to expect, as far as 'action' or, where it would come from next.

Ken Menke and Khe Sanh

The morning convoy, behind our sweep boats, was usually the worst part of the day, for most of us. On the Cua Viet River, at three knots, all lined-up in the channel, we didn't know who was watching from the shore. We had no idea where the mines were and could only trust that the hooks on the sweep boats caught the wires and ripped them out. There was always the notion that we could come under direct or indirect fire anywhere on the trip. That meant, from the time you left the mouth of the river and, until you arrived at Dong Ha, you were a moving target...a damned slow moving target. Then, when you arrived in Dong Ha, you were sitting ducks until you were unloaded.

That gave the entire first trip a very damned good pucker factor. Then, when you add the rest of the day and, part of the evening to it, we spent most of our time on point as well as waiting for something to happen. While we didn't have anything like the Marines did at Khe Sanh...we had our own brand of white-knuckle bullshit.

Ken Menke was a Corpsman; he spent the entire siege of Khe Sanh right there, with the Marines.

This is only important because, Corpsmen aren't Marines and, Marines don't have their own medics. The Corpsmen come from the Navy...they volunteer for that duty...you don't get appointed or chosen, they are given the 'opportunity' to volunteer for it. Ken had joined the Navy after I did then, become a corpsman and, for some reason, volunteered to be attached to the Marines. He spent the entire siege plus a little more with one Marine unit at Khe Sanh.

We didn't talk about it too long so I have no idea which unit it was. He wasn't interested in meeting me or, talking about anything else, so I just let it go, wished him well and hung up.

I was left with a profound sense of sadness.

Around the date I mentioned above, two of our boats were given the job – one day – of picking up a larger force of Marines, coming back from Khe Sanh and, delivering them to a waiting LSD seaside. With them, their vehicles and gear, it took three trips each. My boat, the 913 again, was one of them. I had a 50/50 chance of hauling Ken seaside but, I'll never know. Would we have even recognized each other? Again…I'll never know.

Thing is, we were all getting pretty numb by then. Mentally we were about at the vegetable stage and, most days, operating on reflexes.

What we did try to do was make the trip as pleasant as possible for them. How we did that, was to not rush anything, there was no urgency. That LSD wasn't going anywhere until everyone was aboard. We had cold beer and pop – we got more ice from the geedunk shack, outside of the gate, at the ramp. We brought more beer topside and cooled it (like we were gonna run out?). They were lucky enough to be leaving for a while; we tried to make that pleasant.

When we mated-up to the stern ramp of the LSD, I tried to hold the boat steady enough that no one got their feet wet and, they didn't have to jump. Just step off and walk away.

It was the least we could do…

Rounds!

This was just one of those little amusing things that happened once in a while, we needed something to laugh about anyway.

BM-2 Bacci was a very nice guy, too nice and gentle to be a Boatswain's Mate. I don't know what wisdom got him in Nam and worse in Dong Ha during my tour in '67. Old 'Charles' was raising hell all over the place pretty much whenever he wanted to, no area was really secure and we were always getting shot at on the rivers. Before this time, we had been pretty casual. Now, however we either wore our pots and flak vests all the time or (when at the base in camp) were never more than a quick reach away from them.

Once you made the first trip with the minesweeper and the U-Boats in the morning it was pretty much 'run as loaded'. If you teamed up with another boat Okay, if not you departed the ramp at Dong Ha as soon as you were off-loaded and ran downriver wide open to get loaded again. Back and forth until just before dark. We avoided teaming with the U-Boats at all costs (the older ones) because even though they had some nice firepower they were very slow compared to us.

This was after we finally had radios, nothing fancy mind you but field pack radios that worked...some of the time. Now we would call in before departing either end of the river and get permission from the Ops shack to 'run the river'. We could also call for help and advise them and the other boats of what was happening out there which was a good thing.

Something like three miles upriver from base you made a turn to the left that followed the rivers course to Dong Ha, this part of the channel was about one hundred yards wide and you made damned sure you stayed in the center of it unless passing another boat. For about half a mile you went pretty much straight ahead before turning right, this area had riverbanks that were about ten feet high with very thick vegetation on both sides. We had taken fire from there on occasion for a few weeks, there had been Marines sent in a few days before to clean the area out, but now they were in trouble and being supported by Naval Air and the Air Force. As you went up this channel the area where the action was taking place was on the right, the air support was making its runs from the left.

Bacci had a bladder in his well deck and had been hauling fuel for a few days. I, like most of us, were running mixed pallets of cargo from the ramp. When I backed off of the beach he was probably two hundred yards ahead of me, having one of the fastest boats it now became the usual race to Dong Ha. Yes...you proved you had the fastest boat by racing everyone else, hell we didn't have much amusement!

Besides, if you got there first you got off-loaded first.

Well, by the time we made that left turn into the straight stretch I had cut his lead to just a little over half of the distance, we had a chance to beat him to the ramp. He was about halfway up that channel and I noticed a couple of F-4's were coming in from the left and about to make a run on the area, they would start to unload their ordinance before passing over the river. Bacci was between the heavy vegetation and had no clue that the jets were on their way over.

The reason the jets were hitting that area was a pretty good one for everyone. A few days earlier elements of the 3rd Marines had caught a bunch of NVA regulars moving in, they had trapped them and there had been a pretty intense battle going on. Since we were enjoying some nice weather our guys were enjoying the benefit of some close in air support to help out in the fight. No one knew it then, but this was the beginning of the buildup for the Tet Offensive in our area.

It also looked like he (Baccis' boat) would be directly under their line of attack (insert smiley face). Having fond memories of being bounced by jets on the rivers and almost unloading in my pants a few times I was going to give him a heads-up before they crossed over him, nope. I fumbled for the handset and pushed the button to send…I had turned the thing off to save the battery! While I turned it back on and before I could say anything to him the jets began to unload…yep…he was right under them! The first F4 had opened up with its mini-gun and had probably run it until it was empty, we watched a shower of brass come down like a cloud. I saw the splashes in the river that left a trail to his boat, over it and continued on the other side. The next one was a few seconds behind and did the same thing! About the time I was probably thinking 'thank God for the flyboys' and 'geez hope no one got hurt from all that brass' the radio came to life.

"BASE…SMITTY…817…WE'RE TAKING ROUNDS…WE'RE TAKING ROUNDS!"

That's about the time the next jet made its pass and he got hosed again!

Now I don't blame him for screaming in panic, you are scared shitless when under fire and I had done some screaming into the radio myself in the past.

I quickly checked the river for the splashes of rounds or tracers in the air around the boat nothing...he wasn't under fire.

Someone at the Ops shack screamed back asking for a location in a hurry...there was no response from Bacci so I keyed my handset.

"817...niner one three" and let the button up...a few seconds of silence he replied "what?" in a small voice, no call numbers or anything just 'what?' like he was whispering.

"817...you're taking brass from the planes...over."

The next silence lasted for a good ten seconds or more before he replied in the same way "right...thanks...I know." Then it was our turn to duck as the next few jets made their runs, but we still beat him to the ramp.

Some Days We Did Some Very Good Deeds

The day after the 1475 was hit on that bend in the river, a reinforced company of America's Best was thrown in there to counter-attack and clean out the area. If 'Charles' was allowed to stay there he could raise hell with all of us maybe even sink a boat and block the channel, that would cut our supply line and everyone upriver would begin to run out of critical things like food and ammo after a few days.

The Marines got their asses severely kicked!

Not because they couldn't fight, because old 'Charles' had taken a month to quietly move in and dig in a full reinforced battalion of NVA regulars. These guys were not the ones in the black pajamas either, they were the real North Vietnamese Army, the nasty ones with a cause to drive us out of the country. Not only were the Marines outnumbered about ten to one, but the enemy was very well dug in, they even had bunkers built. Bunkers, the famous 'spider-holes' and tunnels, they had a lot of places to hide and were very well supplied, for the Marines it was a horror show from the get-go. Trapped between the river and the NVA and with no reinforcement they fought!

From the time those Marines made first contact it was one constant fight. We drove up and down the river for three or four days and watched it unfold. During the day there were unending air strikes, at night the sky was filled with flares, tracers, Huey's and a few Dragon-Ships.

In the ongoing wisdom of Vietnam that company never got any reinforcements, they were simply hung out to dry in the bush. Our 'military intelligence' put a company up against what they 'thought' was a company strength force of the enemy in a densely forested area. Wrong again.

Like everyone else (on the boats) we had made our last run of the day and were beached at the ramp at Cua Viet, me and my crew were behind the con getting into some C-Rats and having a few beers for dinner when Smitty appeared in the well deck said "Hey Jon...boat's?" and walked around the con. He had a map in his one hand and a cigar in the other, he didn't look real happy either. After getting all of us real tight he went into it.

"Look, we got a problem and it needs to be done now...no bullshit. I'll show you where and you gotta go pull them out...as fast as you can get your asses up there." He was clearly serious about this. Putting the map down on our little table he pointed with the end of his cigar "Here's where the 1475 was hit...they need you on the beach right here...as fast as you can get the boat there. They know you're on the way and are gonna mark it with smoke."

I was very aware of just where the 1475 was hit as well as was the rest of my crew. We had been passing the 1475 just about a half mile east of the Dong Ha ramp when all hell broke loose that day. That had been the beginning of this battle for Dong Ha about a week earlier. The Marines we were being sent to get were really 'in the shit'.

"Get in…get the Marines on board and get the hell out…you have permission to return any fire to try and suppress the enemy fire and make this extraction." He looked around at us, stuck the cigar back in his teeth and said, "We don't know how many there are…they'll tell you when they get on board. They want whoever is left pulled out…and they want it done fast…'di di mou."

As he left we got a few loaned flak jackets to drape over the con and the gun mount, I fired up the boat and we got into our gear as I backed off the ramp and really put the spurs to the boat…the sun was about two fingers above the mountains as we began to make the run upriver.

When this happened I was 'tickling' my 22nd birthday by a few months. But, we were on our way upriver to rescue some Marines, no problem except for being scared shitless! The loaned flak jackets were to help deflect any fire or shrapnel that was directed at us, the worst part of it was the length of the trip and thinking about what was going to happen at the end of it, the time to think about maybe getting killed. Extra cans of ammo were brought forward for the fifty, extra mags were loaded for the seaman and the snipe striker, there was a lot of yelling back and forth over the noise of the engines as we simply hauled ass upriver.

Most of the yelling was mine. "Look at the target…don't shoot a friendly!"

Something like forty-five minutes later we rounded the turn in the river and saw not only green, but white smoke on the river bank, these boys were using whatever they had to make sure we could find them. I yelled to my 'snipe'/gunner "Hey…don't shoot any friendlies…keep it over their heads!" and got a bobbing head as a 'yes', the seaman and his 'striker' were on the bow (down in the well deck) both armed with M-16's and a bunch of extra mags. I aimed for the smoke, got the ramp down and hit the low riverbank with a thump that about dumped everyone.

We didn't have long to wait, almost as soon as the ramp hit the bank there were Marines running out of the bush, all three of them. Three out of a reinforced company, the one leading ran into the well deck waving me off the beach and yelling "Go...Go...Go!" the other two were right behind him running and ducking.

A few rounds plinked off of us as I yelled back to find out how many more there were to get off, the corporal yelled back "This is it man...go...GO!...fucking go...get the hell out of here man!" A few more rounds hit the boat as I raised the ramp and pulled everything into reverse then ducked down behind the 'big' quarter inch piece of steel that made up the con area.

Backing down very hard the boat shook like hell as we backed off the beach, everyone hit the deck as my 'snipe' opened up with the fifties and literally 'hosed' the bank of the river and anything in the bush behind it until the guns were empty. There was no more 'plinking' as I turned the boat downriver and opened it up literally standing on the throttles.

 We had been the last 'plan' for getting them out, I guess. They were exhausted, worn down and almost out of ammo when we showed up to pull them out. I was glad to make the trip. The only other thing that we could do for them on the ride back was offer them a cold beer and a slug from my good bottle of Johnny Walker. They finished the bottle while sitting hunkered down in the well deck, I didn't care, I knew where I could get another one.

They took it easy during the trip while each put down at least three cold ones, which was the least we could do for them after what they'd been through in the past few days. Our biggest reward was to have each of them shake our hands before walking down the well deck and off the boat, never to see them again.

Refugees and a Little More

I don't really remember when this happened, but I suspect it was just after the monsoon season and Tet of '68. I was back in Cua Viet and things were heating up on the river almost by the hour. If you weren't getting harassed while trying to sleep you got harassed on the river and at the ramp at Dong Ha, the roof had been removed from the con of the boat because we were told it was safer if we took one of those submerged mines.

Now there was no shade.

We were told that Charlie was going to try and sink either one of our boats or an LCU in a narrow part of the river to try and close it to traffic, that made everyone feel real good. The worst part of every day was going upriver in the morning and driving past the bent and overturned hulk of the 821 lying just out of the channel, the boat had been in the channel when a large bomb was detonated right under her. Engines and other boat parts had been found on shore over fifty yards away, but White and his crew were never found. It was a shocking loss and a grim reminder.

What 'Charlie' was doing then was scrounging up our own unexploded (dud) bombs in the DMZ and dragging them down to the river. They could be five hundred seven hundred pounders that were duds for some reason. I mean why should they spend good money on mines when our B-52's made deliveries almost every night?

All they had to do was re-wire them and get them into the channel then wait for us to make the first run of the day...BOOM! If he got lucky there went another boat. We had minesweepers dragging for the wires, but they couldn't catch all of them.

Because of the RPG's/B-40's (rocket propelled grenades) fired at us, we also built what I can only call 'flower boxes' on both sides of the boats. We scared up lumber and using the lifeline stanchions, built these boxes that were four feet high about eight feet long and a foot wide. We filled them with sand. The theory was that if someone fired an RPG at the con these would probably stop it.

In the morning we started out on edge every day, when there wasn't a bunch of U-boats to convoy with you still had to follow the minesweepers upriver for the first trip, it was slow as hell and you felt like sitting ducks out there. You're not only thinking about the mines, but old 'Charles' on the riverbank, a few RPG's, a nice little automatic weapon fire after breakfast, a mortar or just some small arms fire to wake us up. After the second or third trip of the day and nothing happening we all sort of relaxed and just ran cargo.

Smitty showed up on the boat one afternoon and told me that he had a special job for us to do. As he laid it out, I got real sorry that I had ever gone up the Song Thach Han. You see about three miles before you got to Dong Ha the river branched, the one going to the left was the Song Thach Han, this went to Quang Tri city, I had been the only one to run that river so far...damn! Once again 'experience' jumped up and bit me on the ass! While I had never gone all the way to Quang Tri I had been up there to deliver supplies to some Marines and other times made a run to pick up floating bodies of our dead or ferry Marines across the river.

Blood and Brown Water

We all knew that there had been some very heavy fighting in that area in the past few days, units of the 3rd Marine Division were kicking a lot of 'Charlie' ass there and guarding our 'back door' to the south. Our job was simple. All we had to do was go up the river to a place that the Marines would point out and pick up a boat load of refugees then take them to Dong Ha. No one had a good head count, but he said that there would probably be at least two hundred of them, men women and children. The Marines were milling around in front of us, four of them, they had the spot marked and would help us get there, we would also be bringing back a few more Marines that were with the refugees. Yep, just one boat.

Since it was more or less an order we loaded the Marines and borrowed a fifty from another boat to put up forward, it was going to be one slow trip both ways. We didn't run the Song Thach Han much at all so I would have to 'read' it and try to remember from my last trip. As the Marines boarded and we introduced ourselves I felt a lot better, two of them were carrying M-60's and lots of extra ammo, one was the M-79 guy and loaded with rounds, the other was sporting a rocket launcher with a bag of rounds. I liked it better already, these guys were serious, I liked heavy machine guns and now we were carrying five of them, this was good. Just remember kiddies, happiness IS a large caliber fully-automatic belt fed weapon!

The corporal in charge was carrying one of the 60's and he went over the map with me, we wouldn't have a problem finding them, they were pretty much trapped in an open area with a nice big riverbank to land on. I explained that the safest place for them was in the well deck, and it also made a good weapons rest while we made the trip. He agreed and as we got under way they checked weapons and relaxed, my seaman was totally new and seemed to be scared to death. On the way upriver, I told him that he would have the forward fifty. He had been through survival school and knew how to fire one (he said). I remember telling him that if we got any fire to begin firing, but stay low and bring the gun down on the area, look for muzzle flashes and try to target on them. The idea was to keep firing and sweeping a little on the area to suppress the fire as much as possible, hell we were both nervous and I was getting short again. I didn't know about him though.

I had no idea how a green crewman would react under fire.

Everyone was 'on point' when we turned off the Cua Viet and entered the channel of the Song Thach Han, as soon as we entered the river the banks rose on both sides and were covered with dense vegetation, a really good place for an ambush. I was watching the banks of the river so much that I missed the first sandbar, when we came to a sudden stop everyone wound up on their ass except for me! Embarrassed, I backed away, found the channel and apologized to everyone, time for me to pay attention, besides there were enough eyes scanning the banks.

For the next half hour or so, I paid attention, read the river and got us to the pick-up point a little below a place called Tan-Dinh. There was a real crowd waiting on the riverbank. Around two hundred refugees and, no Marines with them. I dropped the ramp and eased in, no one had to be urged, they ran onto the boat flooding the well deck, milling around and looking more scared than we were. Most of them had nothing except the clothes on their backs.

As we waited the corporal came up on the main deck and told me that we should just get under way, the other Marines weren't coming or they would have been there with the people. I backed off the river bank and headed back downriver trying to remember where the channel was, still nervous, but so far nothing had happened.

I had been in country for a while and knew the 'look' of the North Vietnamese. As the corporal hung over the con and we talked, I (for some reason) was looking over our passengers in the well deck. Three of them looked strange as hell and were being avoided by everyone else, they were a little taller and a little cleaner, the hair was a bit shaggy and when you looked directly at them they looked away. I was not the sharpest pencil in the box, but just thought something was 'wrong' about them. As we compared notes the corporal agreed...they were probably NVA deserters. We both figured screw it, someone else could deal with them some other time.

Something like a mile downriver I found out what my new crewmember was really made of. As we rounded a turn and I tried to pick my way along the river going slow as hell we took heavy machine gun fire from the bank, only one person on the boat had time to react as the civilians screamed and hit the deck. Yes, the Marines were up on point, but pointed in all different directions when it happened.

My new seaman (wish I could remember his name) began firing the forward fifty when it was still pointed up in the air, just like I coached him to do. He stood behind it, brought it down and emptied the ammo can into the area that the muzzle flashes were coming from. The fire from the river bank stopped instantly as he swept the area, damn I was proud! The Marines didn't even have time to get off one round until it was over, then just for good measure, the M-79 guy threw a couple of rounds into the area.

It was pretty easy for the M-79 guy to get on target, the fifty had really torn things up and raised a nice cloud of dust there.

As I picked my way downriver, my new seaman finally turned to look at me with a sheepish smile on his face. I gave him the old thumbs-up and we dropped the people off at Dong Ha then headed for home. He became the hero of the day and I hope I pushed him up enough in our group. He deserved it for that. The Marines sent a patrol into that area a few days later and all they could find was blood on the ground, lots of it, but no bodies.

Boot Camp

This is where I should have suspected something, like the rest of my short career in the Navy wouldn't go so good? Boot camp in the Navy is everyone else's idea of basic training, break you down then make a sailor out of you.

I graduated in 1964 with Company 576, Naval Training Center, San Diego, California and I can never forget that number, just like I can't forget the numbers of most of the boats I ran or the number of guys in the outfit that I deployed overseas with. There was something about that number for a company going through boot camp, something in the way it rolled off of the tongue, the way it resonated in the mouth, the way it sounded over the PA system the day we marched by the grandstand and were graduated...just barely.

It was also the hull number of one of the worst piece of shit broken down boats I ever ran. By all rights that boat should have been cut up and sold for scrap.

By the same token my company should have been broken up and sent through boot camp again...and again...and again. We were so screwed up that we made Beavis and Butthead look intelligent...we put the two guys in Dumb and Dumber in the Einstein category! As a company we couldn't do anything as a unit except get in trouble and drive our poor company commander to the brink of suicide. He was almost as harried as the one in that Bill Murray movie, but he survived...just...and retired soon after.

Hell we would be (trying) to march in formation and another company would pass us going the other way, a comment would be passed by them and we would attack, just break formation and start a brawl on the middle of the base.

It got to the point that we either did laundry right after morning chow or after lights out (under supervision) because there had been too many fights (with the other companies in our barracks group) while just doing this one simple thing. The rest of the time we were either drilling, in class, eating or restricted to the barracks, always with a few watchful eyes on us. And...we owned the 'grinder.'

The 'grinder' was sort of a very special place for us. It was about the size of a football field and solid asphalt. This was the place you worked on marching in formation, did morning PT and worked on rifle drill. Company 576 owned it, morning noon and night...and...in the middle of the night. My company would go there just for the hell of it, before morning chow we would stop by and do a few laps to wake us up, and some push-ups to keep us in shape. We could double time to class then go back on the way to lunch...just for kicks then back after the next class for a little more. Before being restricted to barracks for the evening we could go out and do more laps and push-ups and other fun things.

One AM was the best though, the assistant company commander would come crashing through the big double doors at the entrance pick up both shit cans, after turning the lights on and throw them both as far as he could down the aisle between the racks.

'ALRIGHTTTTTTTTT YOU SORRY MOTHERFUCKING ASSHOLES...GET UP AND FALLLLLLLLLLLLLLLLLLLLL IN!'

He actually had a few endearing 'nicknames' for us, mother fuckers, assholes, maggots, dick heads, jerk off are among the few. On a good day he could (as well as our company commander) put all of them together and make a complete sentence that got the point across...without ever using a word that made it sound bad...hell we were used to it!

I think we enjoyed it?

If you didn't wake up right away and leap out of the rack to stand at rigid attention in front of it he had a special way of making sure that you were awake...the whole thing got pulled over sideways and you were instantly awake when you hit the floor.

He was such a nice guy.

Then you would have the pleasure of getting dressed, grabbing your fake rifle and running over to our special 'grinder', hold the rifle above your head and run around it for about an hour until everyone was nice and tired.

Do a few minutes of push-ups just to make sure.

By the time we graduated we had won and lost every pennant that we should have been flying from our guide on, we marched by the grandstand with only our company flag and the 'green weenie'. You get that for just being there thank God or we would have lost that too! This experience should have taught me something.

I Finally Learn How to Run an 8-Boat

To this day I can't remember who the craft commander of my first boat was, he was a nice enough guy. He was only on the boat for about three months then they moved him to an LCU with a promotion to chief petty officer, this change in command gave me the pleasure of serving under BM-1 Horace D. Breeling or Breedland. I say pleasure because he was one hell of a good petty officer to serve under and, had come from the 'Gator Navy'; he could really make an 8-boat perform the way it should. He had run them for years.

I knew that I wanted to learn how to run the boat and, eventually be assigned to my own boat. For this I had to be a 'rated' petty officer, at least E4, which would be a Boatswains Mate, Third Class.

I'd been on the boats long enough to understand how about everything worked and, what it took to handle one. At seventy-two feet long, a twenty-two foot beam (width); fifty tons of boat and fifty to sixty tons of cargo, even with two screws and fifteen-hundred horse power, the first thing you had to do (learn) was to, think well ahead of the boat. The controls were simple, efficient and grouped well. All I had to do was get the necessary experience to work everything together.

The 'Gator Navy' was a term used to identify the boat groups, just like us, who were responsible for getting things ashore or, moving things in the shallow coastal waters – anywhere, all over the world. The sailors who operated shallow draft, flat bottomed boats. The guys who, sometimes, went in under fire or, like us, operated on inland waterways...under fire.

Once I made my desire to learn the craft known to old Horace D., two things had to happen; I had to be promoted to E4 and, for that, I had to pass the necessary qualifications and, the written test. He was happy to take on both tasks. I would handle my normal duties as the boats' seaman, as time allowed, I would study the qualifications manual. As time allowed, my mentor would drill me on the most important things I needed to know, to pass the test. He would be the person handling the manual qualifications for the test.

I'd never been in the fleet; most of the things I should have learned by then, as a seaman, I had never done. On the other hand, being on the boat, for more than a few months, I'd had to learn many of the things. Ole' Horace D would be filling in the rough spots.

Just as he promised and, as often as he could, I was given 'wheel time' in the con. He helped this along by being right on top of me and making things a little harder than they had to be – he made me think about what I was doing. Most of the time, there was also a constant stream of questions.

It didn't stop when I got off the boat; I picked up a following.

There were about two dozen Boatswains' Mates in the group and, almost everyone, had come from time in the fleet. While there were a few that only had short years of experience, most of them had ten or more years of service. That meant that the casual card game, any group meal or a few beers at the club, became 'drill' time. I was an easy target because; I was the only seaman testing for BM3. While things could get intense, most of it was done with some humor. I figured out real fast that most wanted me to pass – they wanted me to sew on that first chevron with the crossed anchors. They beat on me with outstanding good will.

A few weeks later, Horace D showed up with a paper outlining the practical qualifications. Then, during a twelve hour shift, we went over everything and, I passed (everything that could be done on small craft) with flying colors. Next, I took the group test at the White Elephant. That part was so easy that I almost aced it.

While waiting for the scores I was told to braid a lanyard, Horace D gave me the size and added that it should be a four-braid, down to a three-braid then a double. I should use white cotton splice-tie – he even (somewhere) found a small ball of it.

Bosun's pipe/pea and lanyard. The 'Woven Knot'.

When the scores were posted, I think he was as happy as I was. That night, after we took the boat over, for our shift, he presented me with his bosuns' pea and, told me that was what went on the lanyard I'd made. Within a week, he was bumped up to craft commander of an LCU and, I took over the old 913.

Heroism under...'SNAKE!'

One of the worst jobs on a Mike-8, other than changing the batteries, was cleaning out the well deck. We didn't have a pump aboard to use water to clean it out so it had to be swept. Complicating the job of sweeping it was a series of steel 'traction strips', these were something like an inch square and welded to the deck eight inches apart from the rear of it all the way to the end of the ramp. There was a gap left on each side of about a foot and one running down the middle, but you still had to sweep everything to those gaps.

It normally wasn't a big deal, but we had been shuttling 'wounded' tanks and Amtrak's from Hue to a few LSD's for something like a week. We had a buildup of a mixture of that red clay sand and whatever else was on their tracks plus the tracked vehicle that had pushed it aboard. Yes most of them were not under power. Over time this mixture had been piled up and packed down so it was like cement. I'd had the seaman and engineman begin to get some of it out, but it was very slow going. All four of us worked on it one day for a while until we just gave up, we were wearing ourselves out and getting nowhere.

I came up with a plan of attack that was really two-pronged and everyone went along with it but mostly because of the second reason...beer. After telling them to grab some long handled scrapers and fill the cooler with beer and ice I went to the ops shack to tell the chief what I was going to do.

'We're gonna run sea side and catch some swells in the well deck, loosen that stuff up and give it a good wash down.' I told him. His answer was that it was about time we cleaned it out anyway and we had his blessing. By dropping the ramp and running into a swell you flooded the well deck with water, there were four big openings (scuppers) that the water could run back out, as well as whatever we broke loose. The water would also soften it up and make it easier to move, I figured by the time we were out of beer the well deck would be clean as a whistle.

Besides it would lighten the workload and make the crew happy.

While we made the short trip out around the little lagoon and cut through the channel heading sea side I also thought that if I could get enough water in the well deck we could put the boat parallel to the swells and sort of let it slosh back and forth while we rolled from side to side. That left more time to relax and drink beer.

If you looked at some of the pictures you see ones of beautiful blue skies and big puffy fair weather clouds, that's what this day was like, magnificent! Going out the channel the wind picked up to a gentle breeze, we would be running in swells of one to two feet, just enough to give the boat a nice gentle rocking as we rode through them. It wasn't even too hot, life was good.

I got us about a mile out, slowed the boat and dropped the ramp. Everyone was ready with the tools and a beer. When we took the first swell the ramp wanted to float and everyone wanted to jump in and go to work, there wasn't much water in the well deck and I told them to relax, I wanted to get more in and let it work a little. There was no argument.

The next swell was a little bigger. I put power on and pushed the boat into it then raised the ramp. There were a few feet of water in the well deck so I broached the boat and let the swells rock us as the water ran out the scuppers. This was just one of those days that, even where we were, it was a very good day. I messed around continuing to see how much water I could get in the well deck the deck hands walked down there and messed around a little in shorts and bare feet, a few times they walked out on the partially submerged ramp splashing in the water, we were all pretty much kicked back and having fun.

A few times I even caught a big one putting as much as four feet in the well deck and knocking them on their butts, we were all laughing it up for a while and having a very good time. After half an hour of messing around the stuff was coming up pretty easy, we took turns in three's scraping for a while then either myself or the 'snipe' would grab another swell and flush it out. We all agreed that this was a lot easier than doing it the hard way, all you had to do was run one of the big scrapers under the 'gook' and it came right up.

My 'snipe' had just caught a good one and the water was running back out again, he was bringing up a few more cold ones and we were going to trade jobs for a while, we were scraping away and standing in ankle deep water when I heard him yell 'SNAKE!'

I do not like snakes. I'm a snake-a-phobic. Worse if it's a sea snake they are nasty and poisonous! He hadn't yelled it either, he had screamed it! We were out of the well deck quicker than you could say 'snake'. As we stood panting on the main deck looking back into the well deck we realized that what he really meant to scream was 'SNAKES!' lots of snakes! There had to be at least twenty of them and they didn't seem too happy about where they were. They writhed around each other, they swam around and they were trying to get up the walls of the well deck as it emptied. He had accidentally scooped a load of nice green six foot long sea snakes and they were pissed, really pissed! They wanted out and we wanted them out even worse!

Once the well deck was free of water they really got upset!

They weren't going anywhere near the scuppers and I thought about it hard. I was thinking real hard. We had also looked over the sides of the boat and we were sitting in a big nest of them, probably thousands, what a way to mess up a day.

Okay, I was going to get us out of this area before we did anything else, the snakes couldn't get out of the well deck…so far. We would move a mile or so and scoop some more water then hope they followed it out of the scuppers, if they didn't we would have to begin to try and kill them. The only problem with the 'kill them' plan was that all of the scrapers and shovels had been dropped in the well deck when someone yelled snake…not good.

In a steel well deck you couldn't think about shooting them, we'd have rounds bouncing all over the place and someone could get hurt.

I moved the boat a few times and it seemed to work. We'd hit a swell, head on, fill a lot of the well deck with water then back the boat down while it drained. After maybe an hour of this and, staying clear of the large group of them, we had our boat back. We did finish the cleaning job but – with one guy on watch and one eye, of each of ours – watching for more snakes. Yeah, we were a little nervous.

"They are probably going to try and overrun Dong Ha..."

This was sometime in March of 1968. The Tet Offensive was long over, but the entire area around the DMZ continued to be extremely active as far as enemy activity was concerned. The Marine compound, our compound and the ramp at Cua Viet took nightly artillery fire of some kind, Camp Carrol, Khe San, the Rock pile, Dong Ha and everywhere was subject to constant harassment by 'Chuck'. Even though the 'Amgrunts' worked their daily patrols and nightly ambushes, our little 'buddies' simply moved right back in behind them and went back to work.

We could count on sleeping in our bunkers about every other night, being a little nervous while waiting to depart on our first convoy of the morning, really being on edge during that first trip upriver. Wondering if we were going to have some random indirect fire at the ramp at Dong Ha, then a little harassing fire while running the river. Or, taking some kind of fire while being loaded at the ramp at Cua Viet. Did I mention the possibility of driving over a mine in the river...didn't think so.

And people wonder why I'm a little strange today!

'Smitty' got us all together on the ramp one morning before the first trip, it was a simple message. "Ok, here's the scuttlebutt, lissen-up you guys...I want everyone back down here tonight. This is no bullshit…the Jar-Heads say that they have pretty good info that Charlie is gonna try and take Dong Ha."

(That would be about the time we all looked at each other)

He went on, "He's gonna try and overrun the city, maybe the ramp, the airport and everything. We don't want a few of you trapped at the ramp and gettin' shot up or boats sunk…got it?"

Trust me, none of us had a problem with that!

Simple orders, haul as much cargo as possible, but take every precaution to not get caught upriver overnight. Get back home no matter what happens, very easy to understand for everyone. For us it almost worked!

For most of the day my boat hauled nice loads of palletized cargo, easy on…easy off. We made our runs in the normal (mostly) one hour trips, got off-loaded and headed back for more in Cua Viet.

There was no harassment along the river and we tended to relax after a while, sort of, you were still on point most of the time.

On our last run, even before we were off-loaded, a Marine major came aboard the boat. How did I know it was our last run? Well kiddies, by the time we returned to good old Cua Viet and got loaded, we wouldn't have enough time to make another round trip.

The major told me that they had a tank that just had to go to the other end of the river. It was a wounded M-60 that was on its way, being hauled by a 'tank retriever' and should be there any minute. We did have enough time so we waited…and waited…and waited. Should I go on with the waiting?

We were always more than willing to help out the Marines and we did have enough time to load and run, but things started to drag out just a little and to make matters worse the major up and got lost. I finally called in:

"Base 876, over."

"Go 876."

"Base, we have a Marine officer that wants a wounded tank brought back tonight, the tank isn't here and the officer just left...please advise?"

"Roger 876, wait one."

'Wait one' turned into an eternity as he went to find 'Smitty'. We waited while most of the personnel left the ramp except for some security. At that point we had probably an hour and a half to the 'haul-ass' point of departure, my snipe and seaman (we were down to crews of three by then) were huddled close to the con.

We waited...

"876, what's going on 'John'?"

It was 'Smitty's' voice in the handset. Suddenly I felt a little better as I explained the situation. Not great, but better. As we talked I heard the unmistakable sound of the tank retriever's engine roaring down the road, not in sight, but we could hear him. They were big and heavy, they didn't move real fast, but boy were they loud!

At about the same time the major came back down the ramp walking fast, right up the well deck and up to the con.

I explained the situation (to Smitty) and asked what he wanted me to do.

"They are probably going to try and overrun Dong Ha..."

"Get it loaded and get your ass underway, over?"

"Roger," I answered "I know we're runnin' out of time...I'll keep you advised."

One series of (lost) pictures shows a wounded M-48/60 being loaded on a LCU, they (the LCU's YFU's) outweighed us about 3-1. In the pictures the LCU is being pushed off the ramp during the first attempt at loading the tank. It's about the same situation we found ourselves in that night.

I told the major what my orders were, while the tank retriever entered the compound, turned around and straightened up with my ramp. We weighed as much as the 'dead' tank and had lots of 'push' from our two screws. Let the loading games begin!

To totally understand what is happening you must realize that the tank-retriever weighs something like forty tons, those boys are trying to back sixty tons of dead tank into a space that it was just made to fit. The tank is unpowered, but in neutral, hanging off of the retriever on a single cable. It must be backed down the ramp onto our ramp and into the boat...they tried to do the job and almost succeeded. The guy running the retrieving vehicle was good to better at his job!

Even with us at full throttle the first attempt at loading saw my boat pushed right off of the ramp, back into the river. The second attempt was about the same. I had everyone pull away, backed out into the river a little then really beached the boat hard!

I mean I managed to put over twelve feet of our boat high and dry on the ramp. That was the only way we were going to come even close to getting that dead tank on board. I wasn't worried about getting off of the ramp because the heavy-weight retriever could just push us off, that wouldn't be a problem.

The problem was sixty tons of tank that just didn't want to load.

The driver's first attempt got the tank about halfway up the ramp, he sort of wiggled it back and forth gently pushing away while we roared away at full throttle. I could also help a little by changing the position of the boat to the left or right as the tank went crooked. The tracks (or at least one of them) jammed up and the tank went sideways. This was burning daylight too, his next attempt put the tank further up the ramp, but sideways again jamming one of the ramp cables...again no good. By the time he got things straightened up for the next attempt the sun was setting, we were screwed.

It wasn't anyone's fault just a bad night.

There was a quick pow-wow and it was agreed to try again in the morning, the tank was pulled out and parked. The guys in the retriever hauled ass back to the compound, I called in and appraised Cua Viet of our situation. We weren't going anywhere until morning, but they were sending our PBR up for some extra firepower. As we prepared for a long night, I put the boat as parallel to the ramp as I could, dropped our ramp and we began moving all of the weapons into the well deck. We had a nice clear field of fire across the river to the northern part of the city, the same open field of fire up the river as well as an unobstructed view of the bridge. Hell, we were almost under the bridge!

While we got things set up there was some activity down the bluff from the ramp. The Marines moved in a tank, an APC, a bunch of riflemen and a quad-50 complete with a six-by full of ammo for it. It was nice to see that we weren't completely alone!

The bad news was that 'we' were sitting all alone on a brightly illuminated ramp. No, I had asked about it and they weren't going to turn off the lights. We, the boat and the ramp were lit up like daylight. Our PBR arrived (in the dark) and we got together for a little chat, they were going to just meander up and down the river between us and the other side for the night. That made us feel a little better, but not much. We were still a very visible target. I called in for what I figured would be the last time that night, then turned the radio off. It was time to get hunkered down in the well deck and pay attention to the other side of the river.

We sweated we watched and we waited, there wasn't anything else to do. The worst part of anything like that was the waiting. You could talk, crack nervous jokes, check and double check weapons, keep watching and waiting, smoke and have a cold one, but you were still waiting. Totally strung out and on point…just waiting for something to happen. Minutes seem to pass like hours.

The Marines had set up and settled in down on the bluff, we kept an eye on our little PBR in the river.

An 'eternity' later there was movement down by the bluff. A figure came down to the ramp, walked over to the boat, then up to the bow. I met the young lieutenant as he was getting on our ramp.

We exchanged greetings before he said, "Hey, why don't you boys come up on the hill with us? This boat is a friggin' target begging to be shot at, you don't have squat for cover and are fully illuminated down here."

Well gee whiz; I had to agree with his logic.

"Besides," he went on, "if Chuck makes it across the river you can fall back with us, from here (falling back) your asses are totally exposed."

The three of us packed up real fast and took him up on his offer.

As soon as we joined up with them he called in to report that the boat was abandoned. Trust me, we didn't have a problem with that! The three 'River Rats' suddenly felt a lot safer, in good company and weren't as worried about seeing daylight again. Besides, they had nicer 'toys' than we did! We got mixed in on the left side of the outfit, our job was to keep an eye on the bridge and the river around it.

For what seemed like forever, nothing happened. We talked, kept our eyes open and watched our little PBR go back and forth like it was looking for trouble.

About an hour later they found it.

While we waited there had been some scattered activity around us, but nothing close. It was a clear moonless night and almost dead calm. If you didn't look directly at the lights on the ramp your eyes adjusted to the point that I remember being able to not only see our PBR pretty well, but the buildings on the other side of the river. There were lights here and there (in the buildings), but not many. Most of the northern part of the city was dark. The tank was shut down, other than some of us moving around and making very little noise the only sounds came from the quietly idling PBR and the sounds of combat in the near distance.

Our PBR had gone downriver, turned and was just coming back up past the edge of town, about three quarters of the way across the river. At that point someone made a big mistake...some of the 'bad guys'...there were two streams of tracers (one green and one white) fired in the direction of the PBR.

The total fight probably lasted fifteen seconds...okay, maybe twenty.

Our PBR returned fire with everything they had...the quad-50's opened up...every Marine fired and the tank fired one HE round after another, walking them back through the houses. The guy on the quad traversed, very slowly, a few times hosing down buildings on the other side of the river until the order was given to cease fire. Whatever was there had ceased to exist. Everything had been quickly reduced to nothing but rubble; at least a hundred yards beyond the bank of the river.

And...the PBR never took one hit even with all of the rounds thrown at it!

None of my guys even fired a round, we didn't have to. Besides, if we had fired we would have had to clean our weapons the next day.

We did spend the rest of the night in the very good company of some Marines, I don't believe any of us slept much if at all.

The next morning (we had to wait for our minesweepers to arrive) we did have a chance to visit the 'shack', near the entrance of the ramp, run by the Vietnamese family. Our breakfast was probably rice, broth, fruit and a little meat washed down by glasses of tea. As always, inexpensive, very good and lots of it.

The next morning, in under an hour, the tank was pushed right into our well deck. Why had it been so impossible the night before?

Always a lot better than fifteen-year-old C-Rations!

Even if the 'meat' was either dog or monkey, they didn't tell and we didn't ask. It was fresh and good.

Really Riding the Surf!

During my tours I had 'hit the beach' with a few boats, this is a tricky operation when you really are at sea and in the surf. If you screw it up you can wind up sideways and what we referred to as 'broached' on the beach, stuck and helpless. Old Horace D. had taught me how to properly put a boat on the beach and I thank him for that.

The other kind of 'surf' was exciting, exuberating and a real pucker job all at the same time. With a load in the well deck, it of gave you a real rush!

This happened (if I remember right) after Tet of '67 and near the end of the monsoon season, it had rained constantly for a couple of days. It was puke rain that almost stopped operations totally on the Cua Viet River, during this time the river rose about six feet and after the first day was running so fast that our boats couldn't make any headway against the current. When this happened we had to just stop.

When it did stop raining the sun came out for a while and someone figured that since we did have work to do we should try to run the river, one of our guys pulled off the beach (empty) and at full throttle was pushed backwards toward the South China Sea. He did manage to get the boat back on the beach, but it was no easy thing.

For most of that day we just sat around and killed time while the river receded and started to slow down. While we waited, the skies became overcast again and we were treated to a drizzle that didn't stop, there were some periods of rain, but when it wasn't raining it was drizzling. The following day the river had receded a lot, but was still running pretty fast, someone tried again (empty) and could make a few knots against the current, it was time to go back to work. Following that little bit of sun we were now back to that overall sickly gray look to everything, the clouds hung low and dripped.

One of the first things we had to do was take some 'wounded' Amtrak's out to an LSD that had been standing off the coast. They all had some mine damage and couldn't swim out although they could run enough to board us for the trip. We were to take them and their crews out to the LSD drive into it and let them off, pick up the replacement and deliver it back at the ramp. Pretty simple except we had been watching something at the mouth of the river that was just a little unsettling.

Since the river was still high and running fast there was an unusual condition where it met the sea, right at that point was a churning wall of water about ten feet high, and we're going to be driving right into that loaded. Now it is almost impossible to sink a Mike-8, the combination of the water tight 'voids' built into the boat and with the two hatches closed and dogged down (one for the engine room and the other for the after steering area) it's one big-assed tin can. There were also four openings in the bottom of the well deck to let water out of it, even if the well deck did fill with water it would drain out quickly.

The only other openings were the air inlets for the engine room, we figured we could stuff these with rags and seal them up...but...even realizing all of this no one in the group had ever had one of these boats completely under water. From looking at that wall of water and the speed we would be going at it yes, the boats would be submerged at least for a few minutes. A few of us talked it over and came up with a simple plan.

We would stuff the air inlets with rags after turning them to face the rear of the boat, dog the hatch to the after steering nice and tight. We would have to leave the engine room hatch open until the last minute so the engines could breathe, but that could be closed quickly as I pulled the throttles to idle.

I don't know how I got to be the lead boat (probably stupidity), but as we hit that wall of water I would put the engines at idle, the snipe would slam the engine room hatch and stand on it. We would all hang on and wait for the boat to surface. He would open the hatch and we would be underway again...we scrounged up some life jackets just in case.

Smitty and I were talking things over and he reminded me 'don't "broach" the boat'. I had no intention of doing that, but if we lost power the boat would be at the mercy of the surf until we could get the engines started. While this happened we could capsize even with a load in the well deck.

The only thing that we didn't really know was how much of the boat would be under water and for how long, this would bring up one other little problem. Those twenty-four cylinders we were all standing over gulped around twenty-nine cubic feet of air every time they turned over, each engine had a supercharger so the volume was a little higher even at idle. If we were under too long they would suck all of the air out of the engine room and starve...stop. If it came to that and we were without power for even a short time we could broach the boat and that would be a real big 'OOPS!'

My snipe, who took great pride in a clean engine room said 'Don't worry 'Boats', if it comes to that I'll get the hatch open and we can pump out the water when we're clear.' Oh the wonder of being young and confident.

Nervous yep, worse our junior officer decided to go along for the ride so if we screwed up he'd be on our back too!

Approaching that wall of water I yelled for everyone to hang on, the officer was wearing two life jackets and looked like he was going to puke, he was snow white and there wasn't a dwarf in sight. I had everyone stay out of the con and hang onto the rail running around it just in case, if this didn't work I wanted them to be able to jump free.

It actually did work pretty good and happened exactly like we figured it would, boy did we sink! With that Amtrak in the well deck we hit the wall of water and went straight into it, I'll bet we were doing about ten knots, the water came pouring over the ramp, the well deck filled with water and our deck was awash as the water came up to about our knees.

My snipe had slammed the hatch and was standing on it facing me as we went under, I had cut the throttles and probably had the same look on my face that he did, sort of a stupid fearful smile. For a few seconds we sort of wallowed there waiting, with all of the air trapped in the voids we did have a lot of positive buoyancy.

With absolute agonizing slowness, we began to come back to the surface, as the main deck cleared of water (the well deck was still totally full) I nodded to get the hatch back open, we needed the engines because the sea was now trying to push us back into the river. He couldn't, even at idle the engines had sucked most of the air out of the engine room and the hatch was sucked down tight, plan B everyone went to work pulling the rags out of the intakes frantically! He kept straining on the hatch while they did this, as soon as one intake was open I gave the boat a little throttle to keep steerage. In a few seconds he almost knocked himself silly as the hatch came open, I shoved the controls ahead and we were back in business.

My seaman and fireman were happy as hell, after that blast of water our well deck was squeaky clean; they wouldn't have to sweep it for a while!

The trip back was less heart stopping. All I had to do was line us up on the mouth of the river and maintain steerage while we sort of wallowed through that line where the two met then open the engines up and head for the ramp...easy.

After the first trip it became sort of fun!

A Talk with My Mother 2003

'How could you do that every day?' she asked. The answer to her question was as complex as it was simple; it was both hard and easy to answer at the same time. It is at the same time a paradox, but also a pizza cut into eight nice tidy neat pieces, she cried while I tried to explain.

You see...she had no idea where I was in '68.

The other problem was that there was no common frame of reference between us except that she could not imagine what was going on and how it felt to be in the middle of a war, the absolute horrible hopelessness that today may be your last damned day alive.

My mother couldn't even fathom the fact that you just became numb to everything after a while. This happened sometime during my second tour. You get up in the morning and fire up the boat, light a cigarette and have that first canteen cup of C-Rats coffee, followed by something that resembled food in the past. The cig is out of a four pack that was sealed in 1945...your meal is the same vintage...pork and beans and this is breakfast. Your coffee and the meal were heated with a little marble sized piece of C-4 or plastic explosive, it burns very hot and heats everything up nice and fast, it won't explode just heats things up.

My mother received some very ambiguous letters from January of '68 until May of that year; as far as she knew I was safe in Da Nang, how do you explain waking up in the morning and just being numb?

We Meet Our Army Counterparts and Do a Little 'Shopping'

You can't say 'no' to the next day and what you have to do. The most important thing is that your buddies are depending on you as well, as several thousand Marines upriver. You are delivering what they need so desperately every day, every round of ammo, every case of C-Rats...the things they need just to survive.

At night, you forget about a lot until the rockets, mortars and arty (artillery) begin to fall on your position. Most of you spend the night in a heavily built and sand-bagged bunker beside a nice 'hooch' with a 'rack' or Navy issue cot to sleep on. In the bunker you just roll up in a blanket and hide from the rounds coming in while you try to sleep. You can't refuse to run the river the next day and wouldn't think of doing that, you have become numb to everything; you live every day in sort of a heavy gray fog.

You follow the mine sweeper upriver every morning and wonder as you make the slow trip if the grappling hooks they drag will catch and pull the wires attached to the re-wired bombs laying in the channel, denying 'Charlie' a blown up boat in the crisp early morning air. After that first trip you're on your own most of the time, how can you possibly explain to a ninety-four year old woman how it feels to be scared out of your flip-flops and pretty much numb at the same time, how do you explain how helpless you feel when you realize that you are enlisted and committed?

How can you possibly begin to explain the way you intensely scan the riverbanks, but cannot see who is looking back most of the time, the times you expect to be fired on it never seems to happen, when you relax even a little it always seems to happen. You and your crew spend every day at full throttle and on point...just waiting for something to cut loose, nervous as a whore in church. You can't explain that to your mother.

After two years 'in country' you have seen and smelled the best and the worst. You can explain going up a river as far as you could, a point thru pure black still water that nothing moved in, not even the water after a while.

My mother had no idea where I was in '68 and I kept it that way. She would have lost it if she had known that I was up near the DMZ, it was all over the nightly news that the area was getting pounded on a regular basis. What, you write a letter home and tell your mother that 'Hey, today we ran a mixed load of rounds, powder and fuses for the big guns...ain't you proud? Seventh time this week and we didn't hit the lottery yet!'

'Hey mom guess what, we dropped the ramp today and pulled a dead Marine aboard that had been floating downriver for a while! Sure he was all bloated up and stiff as a board, stunk like hell so we got him on the ramp then all went and puked our guts out for a while. Hey, when we grabbed him his skin came off isn't that fun!'

She has no concept of not being able to say no, you can't refuse to do anything.

We have no common frame of reference, no yardstick, she cries and I begin to cry with her after a while. My mother has no way to understand the total hopelessness I felt in '68, actually thinking about a self-inflicted wound to get me out of there. A little shot in the foot.

'How could you do it?' she asks as she cries.

'Simple' I answer 'you can't 'not' do it...there are no options past obeying orders.'

We Meet Our Army Counterparts and Do a Little 'Shopping'

For a few minutes I try to explain what it felt like to go upriver on the first trip of the morning, following those slow-assed mine sweepers while they tried to hook the wires attached to 'our' re-wired bombs laying in the channel. The tension is beyond belief. You are scared shitless, but at the same time sort of calm. You know that if it happens to you, today, it will probably be over before your brain can register it. You and the entire crew will just be dead in an instant.

That is what you call resolve, and the feeling of hopelessness.

When the boat ahead of you or behind you blows up you actually relax. You do feel the great loss for the crew, but at the same time you also feel great relief, sorrow for them, but today wasn't my day to die, maybe tomorrow.

'Charlie' only manages to get a boat once in a while anyway.

How do you explain being suddenly wide awake in the middle of the night? Your eyes are open wide and you are listening to everything around you. You are awake because it is just after a mortar round landed near the compound and woke everyone up; you lay there on the cot and listen. Awake and alert you listen for the sound of the next round…it doesn't happen. This is the one round once in a while to keep us on our toes.

There no others, you just lay there and go back to sleep, no running for the bunker.

'How could you just do that?' my mother asked.

'Because it was only one round' I answered 'nothing to worry about, it missed.'

We Meet Our Army Counterparts and Do a Little 'Shopping'

I didn't find out until a few years ago that the U.S. Army was operating the LCM-8 boats in the Mekong Delta throughout the war. I also didn't realize that (after Korea) most of the LCM-8's had been turned over to the Army. We (the Navy) just 'borrowed' a number of them back to haul supplies in Da Nang and on the rivers up north.

In addition, the reader should understand that this wasn't theft of any kind, we simply 'transferred' some much needed material from one branch of the service to another...us, there was just no paperwork involved in the deal this time.

When this took place things had quieted down a little up north, I would estimate that it was around April or May of '68, there was a general lull in enemy activity (at least on the Cua Viet river) for a while. So quiet in fact that our superiors didn't mind us being stranded upriver at Dong Ha overnight, we didn't mind it either. When stuck up there overnight we could play cards with the local Marines, pick up some good booze from the family that ran the little stand just outside of the gate to the ramp and maybe even score some good weed in the process. They also sold us HUGE chunks of ice to keep our beer cold. When we got real lucky they would share some very good Vietnamese meals with us, hot spicy and delicious, much better than C-Rats!

We Meet Our Army Counterparts and Do a Little 'Shopping'

We had seen the LSD out to sea as we headed upriver this fateful day. We had been told nothing about it (as usual) just sitting there anchored a few miles off the coast. Two of the boats from Cua Viet, mine and (I think Flips) were returning 'wounded' tanks and Amtraks to the mouth of the river. From there they would be cleaned out before being sent back down south to Da Nang. Since most of the vehicles had major (mine) damage they had to be pushed onto the boats, this sometimes took a while. On our last run of the day it was getting late anyway, by the time we were (almost) loaded it was getting dusk. We both knew we would spend the night there.

To our surprise Mike-8's began showing up downriver! These were Green ones, Olive Drab colored...to top that off they had their running lights on!

As they moved closer, then beached on the ramp very nicely, we also realized that these were not only real Army boats but 'Cherry' boats, the ones that had lived aboard a real ship and only did a little part time duty hauling cargo. Some of the things that set this off and us apart, was the total lack of wear and tear, no built-up living spaces or additional equipment that was improvised (like the cabinets and tables most of us had built behind the con), these boats had original 'factory' equipment like lifelines and...life rings hanging where they were supposed to be outside the con. The crews were wearing a thing called a 'life jacket'? What was up with that? These boats had no fenders (old tires) hanging down over the side like we did...and had come all the way upriver with their running lights on while wearing...life jackets? I don't mean a flak jacket...I mean an orange and friggin' white life flotation jacket!

Each boat had two single 50 Cal. machine guns mounted ahead of the con and right behind the well deck on a nice regulation mount. Something else caught the eye of everyone on our two boats as soon as they beached...new 'bronze'!

That is the term used to associate with a screw or propeller, the things under the boats that drove them.

When a Mike-8 is delivered to the Fleet or the Army they have two on the shafts, behind the con there are two mounts for two spare 'screws', one for each shaft. These boats still carried those on those mounts, brand spankin' new 'bronze'! Our boats, even when freshly delivered the first time, had never come with spare props. At that moment of appraisal two 'boat drivers' and two 'snipes' went absolutely giddy! After the amount of time we'd spent chewing our way up and down that river...on and off of ramps in shallow water...getting off of sand bars, catching debris in them...ours were about shot.

Behind the con of each of these boats, coated with grease, were two brand new bronze screws. Sorry ladies, but at that point in time, on that river, this was like seeing a beautiful American girl with great legs in a mini skirt! We became so friendly so quickly that you'd have thought we were the whores!

My snipe noticed something else while I was drooling over the 'bronze'. The rear void covers (on the boat we were checking out) only had four nuts on the twelve bolts used to secure it in place. All of the paint was missing around the bolt holes and the threads were bare, interesting as hell? What was up with that?

In a very 'coy' way we made friends and checked out the other boats, yep, same all over. Spare 'bronze' and the rear manhole cover was in the same shape.

As we did our little (on the sly) inspection we also passed out Cokes, beer, offered whiskey and a little MJ, nothing like meeting the 'troops'? By the time the ramp shut down for the night our new friends had been introduced to the local Marines on security detail, the mama-san running the stand outside of the gate and her daughter. They, the Army boats, had been unloaded (but would be spending the night upriver) and we had our two wounded tanks on board for the morning run down the river. We also had a plan.

The Mike-8 has five 'voids' or water tight compartments between the engine room and the ramp. Each has a sealed 'manhole' on either side of the well deck, which makes the boat just about impossible to sink. The last compartment before the engine room is the largest, you can't stand up in it, it holds the air rams to raise and lower the ramp. It can also be used for 'storage' of gear and vital items. Twenty-four feet wide...eight feet long and 4 feet high...sorta' made us wonder with the paint off the bolts and all...why?

The 'plan' was simple as hell; these guys had been aboard ship and not used to alcohol of any kind for months, simply get them drunk and passed-out! Once they were 'down' we could go exploring and have some fun, maybe even find some things to use besides the 'bronze' they were carrying around? We found the 'Mother Lode' that night. Being very nice and 'social' we helped them drink and smoke until they began passing out, one by one they bit the dust until all of the crews were snoring in their life jackets very soundly...with a few pipe wrenches and crescent wrenches our crews went to work on the boats...it didn't take long.

What we found in that last void that night was like opening King Tut's tomb!

While a couple of seamen (quietly) unbolted that 'bronze', on two of the boats, and moved it to our boats we grabbed flashlights split up in two teams and got into the voids. We had suspected that we would find some spare parts stowed down there, we were pleasantly surprised to find a lot of things that we had been doing without because we were always told 'it' wasn't available from supply!

They had brand new 50 Cal. machine guns broken down in the original factory boxes, wrapped in that semi-transparent stuff and coated with Cosmoline! All we were interested in were a few spare gun barrels, they could keep the rest of the parts. As we dug through things we came up with filters, belts, hoses, camshafts, complete injector pumps plus lines and gaskets for the engines and transmissions! Those boats were floating parts stores! Since we knew that they weren't based 'in-country' and, if they broke down would be in a position to be repaired, we didn't feel bad about relieving them of some of the things. Believe me, if they had been based 'in-country' we probably wouldn't have touched anything, this was totally different.

For about an hour we 'shopped' the two boats passing things out of the voids and onto our boats to stash all of the goodies in our engine rooms and after steering spaces. We worked quickly and quietly then replaced the manhole covers and nuts just like we'd found them. The only thing I remember wondering about just then was if they would notice the missing 'bronze' in the morning. We couldn't make our 'getaway' until our minesweepers got to us on the first trip upriver, that would have them walking around on their boats for a few hours. Longer if the mouth of the river was fogged-in. If we got caught we would have to give the screws back and we really didn't want to do that! Oh, and the only place we could hide them was in our well decks, the guys had worked their butts off sliding them under the two tanks while we'd been raiding the voids. They wouldn't fit through either of the hatches to be put out of sight below deck.

We did get lucky. The next morning was beautiful clear and sunny, the Army boat crews had massive hangovers so they weren't functioning very well. So far so good. When I turned the radio on I was greeted by the normal chatter from Cua Viet, they (the morning convoy) had left and were underway for Dong Ha, if all went well and there were no problems during the trip in about two hours we'd be going downriver. Believe me, we worked at being even nicer to them that morning and kept them as occupied as possible. That included fresh coffee, breakfast and anything else we could do to keep them busy. It helped that some of them were in the engine room's part of that time checking things out prior to firing the boats up.

When our minesweepers appeared around that last bend in the river, there was probably one huge collective sigh of relief from the six 'thieves' on our boats! It finally looked like our little shopping spree would go un-noticed. As we bid our Army friends goodbye, shook hands all around and wished each other well in the future, we offered to lead the way back down the river. I still couldn't believe that none of them had noticed the missing screws until then!

Blood and Brown Water

As the other boats got closer, we all fired up engines backed off of the ramp and gave the arriving convoy a clear place to beach. Our minesweepers turned for home as we formed up and prepared to outrun them in the first mile. One of us made the call to base that we were underway with the Army boats following us. We had to make that trip a little slower because those 'regulation' boats still had the engine governors hooked up and we could have easily outrun them too.

The new 'bronze' was kind of hard to hide so we passed the word that there would be at least one or maybe two new screws available after our worst one(s) were replaced. As I remember I did have to have both of mine replaced and boy did that ever smooth out that boat! I think the other guy only really needed one. To this day I still can't believe that we pulled that one off so well! We didn't think that the spare parts from 'voids' would be missed for quite a while, maybe never, but four screws that were three feet in diameter, almost ten inches in pitch, sitting right out in the open behind the con of those boats? Give me a break!

Ok, it could have been that, given the situation, maybe no one cared or just overlooked the fact that they were missing.

On the other hand, just maybe, we could have asked for them? But why take the chance of being turned down...right?

Ship Ahoy!

There were always ships just off the coast cruising up and down, destroyers, frigates, cruisers, then later on the battleship New Jersey. They loitered around out there waiting to get a firing mission somewhere inland to support our troops, most of the time we were too busy to go 'begging', but every so often one of our boats would be lucky enough to be downriver and for some reason off duty.

In a place like Cua Viet this combination of a boat being idle, a destroyer being close to the coast going slow and someone seeing it set things in motion quickly!

We had no chow hall and nothing that resembled a 'club'; our meals were either C-Rats or what we bought from the locals to supplement that. At times we would raid a pallet of canned food we were hauling, most of this stuff was dried something or other, we opened it added water and waited then covered it with hot sauce so that it was edible.

There were pallets of cases of canned fruit once in a while, we really raided them.

When a ship showed up that we thought we could get close enough to hail believe me you got permission to go sea-side in a hurry! If you couldn't get the Ops shack/bunker on the radio you sent a runner from the boat while you warmed it up and got ready to leave, you did this and prayed that you weren't needed upriver.

Ship Ahoy!

As soon as you had permission you hauled-ass! Then prayed they didn't get a fire mission before you caught them.

If you were lucky enough to catch the ship then lucky enough to be allowed to send someone aboard it was like Christmas, in most cases we were not turned down, in some cases (after chasing the ship down) they would get a fire mission and we got left behind. That was always a big letdown. It also was not just as simple as 'driving' out to the ship.

Above I used the term 'loitering'. A ships loitering speed in the ocean was about as fast as we could cruise and they were somewhere between five and eight miles off the coastline. Once we were in the South China Sea, as opposed to being on a calm river, we were going slower as we ran through the swells. The idea was to head out like you were 'shooting' at a moving target. You would get picked up on radar or by a lookout sooner or later, identified as 'friendly' and the ship would slow down a little. They could never stop, but they could slow down long enough for you to get there and try to do some creative 'begging'. Usually it didn't take much, they had a pretty good idea of what we wanted and gave it without us even asking, many times the cooks or storekeepers would suggest things we hadn't even thought of.

As you got close enough to the ship to be heard you hailed it by yelling at the top of your lungs requesting permission to come alongside, if you got a wave from the bridge you by God popped a nice snappy salute in that officer's direction and held it until it was returned! The other thing that made this transaction interesting was that you couldn't tie up to the ship, in most cases they had the gangway stowed or put away since they were at sea and had no use for it. Once you were alongside and bobbing like a cork beside the bigger ship you yelled for permission to come aboard then waited to get the okay from the bridge again. We looked pretty ragged most of the time and they knew where we had come from so that was usually not a problem either, by that time the railings would be lined with some of the ship's crewmembers checking us out, taking pictures and waving. If no one on your crew wanted to make the jump to the ship you did it yourself. Normally your snipe would take the controls because he would be the only other one on the boat with enough experience to handle it under these conditions. The ship is going up and down in the water a little, but you are close to its side and riding right on top of each swell...then going down as much as six or eight feet as it passed under your boat. And that would be on fairly calm day.

The older destroyers were the easiest ones to board, anywhere astern of about amidships because they rode lower in the water, at the top of the swell you could 'almost' step up onto the deck...almost. I'm sitting here typing this now thinking back...HOLY SHIT!...I could have been killed! Oh well, young, dumb and the lure of fresh anything.

The ship and your boat are both moving up and down in the ocean, your boat is bobbing alongside like a cork riding the swells.

Your snipe is trying to hold the boat alongside without smacking the side of the ship. Yep...all this steel is also moving side to side, you're a foot away then five feet away. The best place to board from is all the way forward on one of your gunwales.

You wind up riding your boat while standing on a piece of steel that's a little over a foot wide, with no handrail or lifeline to hang on to. The joy of being young.

If you miss you're gonna either fall into the well deck of your boat or between the ship and your boat, I don't remember ever actually thinking about that possibility. I also wasn't thinking about the two HUGE screws turning slowly under the destroyer or the ones turning faster under our boat, I could have either been crushed or chopped into fish bait! Nope...at times like this we only had one thought on our minds, fresh anything!

What life jacket?

You time it then make the jump grabbing one of the lifelines and getting a foot on the deck, in most cases there are a few guys more than willing to make grab for you, just in case you're a little off target.

Then...Welcome to Heaven!

If you had made your intentions known in advance (by yelling back and forth), there was stuff being carried up from the galley or store room as you got on board. There were lots of willing hands moving things over by the rail and there was usually a cook either asking what all you wanted or directing a bunch of seamen to help out. On a good trip we wound up with cases of fresh fruit, veggies of all kinds, big cartons (five gallon size) of milk, fresh meat and the crown jewel, ice cream! Normally 'if' you were even offered ice cream you didn't ask for a special flavor. You took what you were given and appreciated it, hell we would grovel while thanking the cook for it!

One of these begging runs that really stands out in my mind was going alongside a newer destroyer. The cook that gave us the stuff probably got strung up from the yardarm! Not only were we given both white and chocolate milk, but he threw in both flavors of ice cream. Then, as he passed another big container to me, patted the top of it with affection and said, "Peach sherbet...from the officer's mess," with a smile and a wink. That was the mother lode, but he wasn't finished! He asked me how many guys were in our outfit and I tried to count heads in my mind as quickly as possible "About forty." I answered. Turning to a big black seaman in a cooks white uniform he said something that I couldn't hear over the noise around us, when the guy came trudging back I could have kissed him, he was carrying two cases of frozen steaks!

My crew became heroes for a week.

When they started hauling stuff out, you thanked everyone around you and worked fast, passing it to the waiting hands on the boat. My guys didn't have to be told to get moving. They knew that we couldn't handle this stuff in a casual way, at any moment this ship could be given a fire mission and would have to get under way immediately, if that happened you jumped for the boat. In most cases you passed everything across, thanked all of the guys on the ship, saluted any officers that had gathered and timed your jump back aboard the boat.

The one thing you NEVER forgot to do as you pulled away was to face the wing of the bridge that either the ship's captain or executive officer was watching everything from and give him your best salute of undying gratitude. Not your little 'there-have-one' hit your head with your finger and drop it, no way, you faced him, came to stiff attention and held the salute long after he returned it. Then you held it and faced the crew, some waved, some saluted back, even the enlisted men. After all, they really didn't have to give you anything and you appreciated it.

When we got back we shared what we had with everyone else.

Ship Ahoy!

There was one time that I almost re-joined the 'real' Navy for a while.

We had made a run at a destroyer that was a little too far out, I had noticed after we chased her for a while that the ship had made a little change in course and was moving away from us slightly. The sea was pretty calm so we continued our run and were gaining a little, once we were spotted the ship did slow quite a bit and let us catch up, it took over an hour to finally get alongside.

After all of the usual transactions I had the guys stand by while I went to the ships store for a carton of cigarettes, in the time it took me to walk the fifty or so feet I felt this sort of low rumble under my feet. A few seconds later the intercom announced 'Battle Stations…All Hands Battle Stations Guns! All Hands Man Your Battle Stations'…oops!

That rumble I felt were the turbines starting to spin up, the announcement meant that they had a fire mission…the combination of the two meant that the captain probably didn't know I was still aboard!

I did a quick about face and almost ran right into a young officer. His face instantly took on the expression of "Oh Shit…this ain't right!". He turned and I followed him to the closest intercom. He picked up the handset as I took a quick look aft, yep my boat was getting left in the dust. There was a hurried conversation with the bridge, before it was over he asked me "How fast can your boat go?" I answered and he relayed that to the bridge then (after a pause) told me "The skipper is going to stop engines for just a second…you have to make a jump for it off of the fantail." Like I had a choice?

He stopped the engines, but didn't stop the ship. My snipe kept the boat at full throttle, but was catching up very slowly so I got to the fantail where they could see me and pointed to a spot directly under it. Then, facing the wing of the bridge popped the skipper a nice salute before looking aft again, the boat was getting closer.

Using hand signals I showed him that I wanted him to go across the stern of the ship at an angle, there was no way I was making a jump onto the cluttered deck or maybe miss and wind up five feet lower in the well deck. We still had covers over the con areas then, they were two by four frames with half inch plywood over that. From what I could figure the roof of the con would be about four feet away and about five feet below me, a nice big open spot to land on, I also had our mast to grab. I didn't want to bounce off into the South China Sea either, big damned sea snakes and you never knew where they were!

Another 'snipe' made me proud of his boat handling skills! He got the boat within about six feet and backed down real hard to match the speed of the destroyer, I had been standing outside of the life line holding on and waiting. All I had to do was let go and push off a little, my 'go-aheads' hit with a 'slap' and I was home! They went back to speed as we turned for home giving the crew our heartfelt waves of thanks, damn I was still going to be smoking C-Rats cigarettes for a while.

There was one 'forbidden fruit' in Cua Viet…apricots.

Not only were canned apricots one of the C-Ration side dishes, but there were times we found entire pallets of them being hauled by us. This sort of falls into the strange but very true category of all things Vietnam.

Ship Ahoy!

Apricots are good; we all know that, they were also the 'forbidden fruit' up north because they were a 'round magnet'. Open a can of them and you would be guaranteed to begin receiving incoming rounds of some kind within minutes...if not seconds!

You could eat them on the river...you could eat them in Dong Ha...hell you could eat them almost anywhere...except Cua Viet. I have been in a bunker hunkered down long after the last round came in, I mean long after! I have heard a P-38 pierce a can of something because someone was hungry...had the aroma of apricots fill the humid stinking air in the bunker as the can was opened and some 'cherry' took the first one out. Listened to the groans of a few others in the bunker as they caught the familiar aroma. Then cringed as the first round came whistling in overhead.

Cua Viet and apricots were never meant to be together!

Hitch-Hikers and Other Passengers

We hauled a lot of passengers on the rivers, in most cases we were the fastest way to get either inland or somewhere down a river. Our boats hauled the worn-out battle weary Marines away from the fighting for a little R&R, we hauled the fresh ones back in to replace them. We hauled their vehicles both ways. Same thing, new ones in, worn out or 'wounded' ones out.

We all had the same look after a while. That dull expression, flat smile (when they did smile) with little joy in it. There was some joy in the fact that you were still alive. There was one other thing we shared with them on every trip, being just plain mad, especially the ones going out riding with us down a river. You saw and felt it as soon as you got underway, everyone was 'up' and 'on point' alert and ready...also pissed-off. My guys were that way because we were tired of being screwed with most days (and nights), the Marines were that way because they had been through a lot worse. They still wanted to kill; they were looking for revenge. A chance to even a score.

When the boat backed away from the ramp, they were checking weapons and watching the river banks just like my crew. 'C'mon 'Charlie', screw with us just one more time.' After Tet of '68 you didn't relax much during a trip on the Cua Viet river, it seemed that even when doing something else that had you occupied you were still looking around and 'on point'.

We carried 'spooks' (CIA) quite a bit when up north, there was one that I saw every few months when he was going back in and needed a ride. His uniform was not quite a Marine or Army field uniform, he wore nothing that identified him in any way. He was heavily armed and very quiet. When my boat was about to leave he would walk on and ask if he could ride along, at the other end of the trip he would thank us for the ride and just disappear.

We hauled refugees around, ARVN (South Vietnamese Army) troops, advisers and just about anyone that needed a ride. It was all part of the job.

Last year I got one of the shocks of my life. I met 'Zeus'. I had delivered him and his Seal Team to a point in North Vietnam in the middle of the night over thirty years before. It happened by accident and as we stood talking about it I got a real case of chills. We took them in, dropped them off and I never knew what happened after that. We just forgot about it and went back to work.

Lynn and his wife Vicky own the motel that a group of us stay at in Lake Lure North Carolina, they are very nice people and work to make our stay as nice as possible every year. A few days after we were there a bunch of us were standing around in the bar in the afternoon after returning from a ride. I have a patch on the back of my vest that reads 'Jane Fonda, American Traitor Bitch'. Someone walked up behind me, tapped the patch a few times and in a deep but soft voice said, 'I like your patch.' I turned and had to look up into Lynn's grinning face. We talked for a while.

In 1968 he had been dropped off just above the DMZ in North Vietnam by a Mike-8. As the conversation went on we both realized that it had been my boat, as the boat driver with the most experience (God I hated that word!) I was selected to make the trip.

We were going in 'bare' too, just one boat and no cover. The only thing we could count on was being as quiet as possible and if we ran into problems there was a destroyer on call to give us supporting fire.

The chief caught me after my last trip of the day explained what was going on and we went over a map for a few minutes. I would load them after dark then go out to sea a few miles before turning north and running for a certain time at so many revolutions, which would get us above the DMZ to an approximate landing area. The idea was to get them on the beach 'dry' wait a few minutes to make sure there wasn't a 'welcoming' party then get the hell out of there and back, once their boots hit the sand they were on their own unless there was a reason to pull them back out. We would turn around put the 'spurs' to the boat, get a few miles off the coast and run back south, there would be no radio contact at all, 'Zeus' and his team would handle all communication if it was necessary.

The chief also said 'Oh…once they hit the beach stick around for a few minutes…just in case you have to extract them…ya' know…if they run into some opposition and have to pull out.'

They were used to this stuff, we weren't. Yes, we were on edge and really 'on point' for most of the trip! It was a clear moonless night, very calm and there wasn't a lot of surf. As far as everyone knew, the beach we were going to put them on was clear of sandbars or any other obstacles. As far as they knew. We got loaded, introduced and there wasn't much conversation after that.

By the time we cleared the mouth of the river my eyes adjusted to the darkness, I put us a few miles out then turned north, checked my watch the revs and watched the compass. The only light was the glow of my instruments and the fading lights of the AOG moored to the buoy near the river. After a while they were just a dim glow on the horizon then faded to nothing behind us, we were alone and headed north. My snipe and me covered most of the instruments (except the compass) after a while, the glow was an annoyance I had to be able to 'read' the swells, find the beach and try to see the surf where we were going to land.

At the end of my timed run I made the turn toward North Vietnam, slowed the engines to just a little above idle and wished the hell we had better mufflers on them. They sounded like a brass band and the 'burbling' sound they made as the boat dipped (putting them under water for a few seconds) I was sure could be heard all the way to Hanoi! After a while I could see the whitecaps breaking on the beach. I wanted a cigarette so damned bad, but we didn't dare smoke. We let the Seals know we were just about there. We got closer, I just kept enough power on to maintain control of the boat as I tried to pick my wave to ride in to the beach. You are 'surfing' a fifty-ton boat in, the idea is to try and pick a small one then ride just at the crest of the wave until you get in close, back down just a little and let it 'lay' your bow on the beach.

Try doing that at night. Kep the boat square with the wave-front so you don't get sideways and 'broach' the boat, stay just behind the crest of it and wait for it to begin to break. Watch the waves breaking in front of you to try and judge how far you are from the beach, hope that the charts were right and you won't wind up sitting solidly on the bottom when you land. If you do get stuck it's your problem, the Seals have their own job to do and you're not supposed to be here anyway. Pass the word to hang on, here comes the beach.

I was pretty proud of myself, I had picked a good easy swell to ride in on. As it began to break there was only something like three ahead of it so the beach wasn't too shallow after all. When the other whitecaps disappeared I backed down slowly and we made a nice smooth landing, it was nothing like the 'train-wreck' I had worried about. I had been nervous for most of the trip now, as I dropped the ramp on the sand of North Vietnam I was just plain shittin' bullets! Right, we were supposed to hang out there for a few minutes and make sure they didn't need a speedy trip back off the beach! That and the fact that our exhaust noise would get louder as we left, they were gone as soon as the ramp was down fading off into the night like so many dark shadows, we sat there bobbing in the surf a little idling ahead while the waves smacked the boat in the butt. I was positive that at any second a whole battalion of NVA was going to come storming down the beach and attack us.

Nothing happened, there was just the noise of our exhaust and the surf while we waited for a few minutes, tense and really on point!

With great relief I pulled the controls into neutral then reverse, the ramp came up as we began to slip slowly off the beach and back into the South China Sea and darkness. As soon as I thought there was enough water under the boat to make a turn I spun the helm and used the engines to pivot us around then opened the boat up slowly, there had been no firing on the beach and we were out of there at just a little above idle speed.

For probably ten minutes we hammered through the small swells at a slow but quiet speed, putting as much distance between us and North Vietnam as we could before turning south. As I made the turn I put the 'spurs' to the boat and we began to relax. In a little while the glow of the lights from the AOG were in sight again, now we could turn our running lights on so someone didn't take a shot at us!

It was time to flip that old Zippo open and light one, we could relax.

'Zeus'/Lynn told me how much he and his team appreciated the good soft dry landing, they weren't sure how it would go. I had to tell him that it was more luck than anything else. Sure, I had beached in the surf before, but never on a pitch black night, as far as I knew none of our guys had ever done that before. After over thirty years he complimented my crew on a job well done.

He also told me what happened and why they made the trip. They were sent to grab an NVA officer that was pretty important, they did get him, but it wasn't all that easy. Once they had him things got pretty hot and they spent the next week dragging him around and trying to evade the NVA searching for the team, this and working their way back across the DMZ and safety. Our job had been a cake-walk compared to his.

We also picked up 'strays' once in a while.

Heading up the river one day (from Cua Viet to Dong Ha) we noticed movement on the northern bank, there wasn't much there but tall grass. As we got closer a figure stood up and started to wave his arms frantically above his head. He was big, black and in a Marine uniform. He also wanted our attention in the worst way! I slowed the boat and aimed for his position on the shore while the crew really became alert! As we got closer a smaller figure stood up beside him, these guys were like Mutt and Jeff. The black guy was over six feet tall and his little white buddy was about five foot six, I pulled in and dropped the ramp. They literally ran aboard and I thought I was going to get kissed!

They were missing a lot of equipment, but still had the important things. The black guy was carrying an M-79 grenade launcher and a few remaining rounds for it. The important thing was the ammo he was carrying for his buddy, the one with the beat up M-16 rifle. They were still high on adrenaline and very glad to get picked up. They told us the story as we shared water and food with them.

Their platoon was doing recon south of the DMZ and had laid up for the night. It seems that while they tried to get some rest while listening for 'Charlie's' movement in the bush something like a company of NVA began moving right through their position. The one guy said that it seemed like they were 'sweeping' or looking for the platoon.

We also picked up 'strays' once in a while.

Suddenly there was contact and all hell broke loose on all sides, when this happened they were almost completely surrounded by NVA. From what they said the beginning of the firefight was as chaotic as it was ferocious, it did die down after a while to occasional encounters, but in the chaos the platoon became separated and disorganized. These two had been together in the beginning and had stuck together all night through the heavy on and off fighting.

At dawn contact was broken and when they realized that the platoon was very scattered, they began to make their way to where they thought the river was. They had no idea of what they were going to do when they got there. These two very tired Marines rode with us to Dong Ha, thanked us for picking them up then went to find someone to report to. Two very lucky guys.

We also had the pleasure of transporting an Australian USO troupe once. I don't know why they couldn't be moved by air, we picked them up in Dong Ha and took them as far as the base at Cue Viet. None of us minded that trip one little bit! The girls were young and pretty, they were wearing 'Hot Pants' and 'Go-Go' boots! They were even nice enough to put on a little bit of a show for us on the trip downriver and pose with us for pictures...that made the trip worthwhile! We passed around a few cold beers on the way down and I remember one of these cute girls downing about half of one, then belching like a sailor. She blushed then excused herself for 'bad form' by then we were all laughing like crazy, it was nice to meet a normal 'round-eye' girl.

I think I felt the most for the Marines we hauled. After all, they were the first ones in and the last ones out. I remember looking them over as we pulled them back, taking them out to an LSD to return to either Da Nang or somewhere else they were going. These guys were filthy dirty, torn up and just plain worn out. You could see it on their faces the way they carried themselves and the way they moved, there was no fighting for 'Mom's apple pie' or 'Old Glory', they had fought like hell just to stay alive for the past few days. Numb and fatigued they were pretty well drained of all emotion except sorrow and 'pissed-off'. In most cases if we had something good to share with them like fresh cigarettes, candy or just some good food we had, the same went for beer, booze and fresh 'Mary-Jane' if we had it. We offered and didn't get turned down too often, it was the best 'perk' we could offer them, the Marines we hauled out were the lucky ones...they were still alive.

It was an odd thing to watch too, on the trip downriver, they knew that it wasn't over yet. There was still the chance that we could get hit before we got to the end of the river and went sea side to the waiting LSD we were delivering them to. We (myself and my crew) were 'on point' during the trip. Almost always at least half of the Marines were too. While some of them just flopped in the well deck resting, the others were standing, resting against the sides and scanning the river banks, weapons ready.

Taking a fresh company or battalion ashore to replace them you tried not to look at the faces, but you had to. Clean and fresh off the ship they were nervous and anxious, except for the older officers and sergeants they were our ages or younger. Most of them couldn't buy a beer in their hometown, but they surely could die three thousand miles from it.

I spoke about the worn-out ones above and further up about how we all just sort of felt 'pissed-off' most of the time. You get that way after a while when you are trapped in a frustrating futile situation

We also picked up 'strays' once in a while.

that seems to have no ending and certainly no clear meaning. A lot of the guys around you have died fighting for a piece of worthless real estate that you will abandon and give back tomorrow or the next day. Or worse...you will be told to defend and hold that place at all costs. At least when the heart was cut out and all hope was given up you still had 'pissed-off' to fall back on.

A good example of that would be (the remains of) a company of Marines that we were taking downriver from Dong Ha one day. A normal company is made up of eighty men. There were twenty of them (more or less), no officers and no sergeants. As a unit they were ragged, dirty, torn-up and tired. The company commander was a corporal about my age.

These Marines were bone weary after being in the bush for over two months, worn out and worn down from constant combat. They still had two things going, spirit and pissed-off. We had a few things to help most of the time. Weed and papers if they wanted that, a good bottle to pass around during the trip and always...cold beer and Cokes.

As we came around a turn in the river we were ambushed, there was a lot of fire from one place on the river bank and a few RPG's were fired in our direction. The Marines had been relaxing a little. As a unit they rose in an instant to lay down return fire on the position, before we could get our weapons firing they were pouring it back in and they were laying it on heavy. Some of them actually fought for a firing position along the side of the well deck with their buddies.

Within seconds the well deck was littered with bouncing rolling brass ammo casings, belting from the two M-60's and brass casings from the M-79s.

Blood and Brown Water

The RPG's missed and there were no more, the Marines kept firing even after the fire from the shore had stopped. A cloud of dust rose into the calm hot afternoon air on the river bank as empty magazines were ejected and replaced by full ones. I suppose the clearest way to explain the feeling came from the one M-79 guy in the company, he loaded one more round snapped the weapon shut shouldered it and fired. We all watched as it clearly exploded right on target...he was good!

He had watched the impact like the rest of us, but said, 'Take that you 'Charlie'-Motherfucker.' He said it in a flat even tone with no emotion involved, broke the weapon and popped out the casing adding to the litter in the well deck. Because of the exhaust noise I didn't really hear him say anything. I read his lips and understood what he had said. He wore no 'pot' and didn't scream it out, he said it turned and leaned against the side of the well deck to hang his head as he slid down and sat in total exhausted frustration.

Some days 'pissed-off' was a good thing.

The 'New' Chow Hall in Cua Viet is Opened and Closed in Less than Five Minutes.

This was one of the times that the enlisted guys had far more brains than the officers that assumed to lead us or boost our morale were born with. We all seemed to understand that this, the nice new chow hall, was just something we didn't want anything to do with. Why? We were all a little nervous just using the latrine or being in the hooches at night.

In Cua Viet if you stayed in one place too long (unless it was in a bunker) you listened for the sound of incoming rounds and got a little jumpy. Even the simple and very personal task of a trip to the latrine was well planned in advance.

Go ahead and laugh about that, but it was true. First, make sure it's not a false alarm like you just have gas. Second, find paper. Third, scout things out by making sure it's either empty or there is only one head sticking up. We had a 2-holer with sandbags built up to about shoulder height so if it was occupied you could see that. You did not walk over there and stand in line...trust me. Fourth, move out, get over there, get things accomplished and get out!

To us, at least, it (a chow hall) didn't seem to make too much sense. Why put everyone in one place for about an hour a day (or a few times a day) and give 'Charlie' time to take a shot at us? We all knew

The 'New' Chow Hall in Cua Viet is Opened and Closed in Less than Five Minutes..

from experience that 'he' could get real close to the target after a few rounds of anything, why make ourselves willing targets?

Yes, we were all pretty tired of C-Rations, but we weren't tired of living.

Besides, by late winter/early spring in 1968, we had eaten out way of the 40's era of C's and into the early 50's. They were getting better, fresher and the meal we disliked the most was gone...finally! That would be the Ham and Lima Beans.

The SeaBees built the new chow hall while we hauled cargo to keep the war going in our part of the country. We, the boat crews, talked about having a meal there and pretty much agreed that unless it was heavily sandbagged (roof and all) we weren't interested in it. Military food wasn't that great so why tempt fate to have a so-so semi-hot meal of something you probably couldn't identify anyway.

I do remember that day well, when we had been downriver loading there were a few Huey's landing dropping off 'brass' for the big ceremony and the official ribbon cutting for the evening meal.

On our next to last trip (our day was cut short so we could all be beached at about 4 PM to attend the ceremony), I bought a freshly butchered chicken from one of the Mama-San's at the Dong Ha ramp. We would be eating that, some greens and whatever else we could 'scrounge-up' for dinner...on the boat.

I pushed the boat hard up on the beach shutting down the engines for the day, my crew made a run for the hooches to grab some extra gear. While they were gone I got the chicken out then began to cut it up on our little table area behind the con.

Blood and Brown Water

It was a very beautiful late afternoon in Cua Viet. Almost no wind at all, an air temperature of probably eighty-five degrees, pure blue sky with only a very few small puffy white clouds. I began using my K-Bar cutting the chicken up into pieces that would fry up easily in our little frying pan, my only 'war' just then was going on with the flies that wanted to carry it all away. As I worked I poured some oil into the small skillet we had then started making marble sized balls of C-4 for frying it up.

However, even as I worked at dinner and opened another nice cold beer I was 'on-point' as always. I didn't have long to wait.

I lit the first 'pill' of C-4 to begin to heat the oil in the frying pan. While it came up to temperature I pushed the chicken pieces around in the flour/salt/pepper mix to get them ready. We were pushed up on the beach/ramp at the end of all of the other boats...everyone else was gone.

I heard the first round coming from across the river it was a very low sort of 'whomp' sound when it left the tube. When it went off about 50' behind the boat I froze looked around at the fountain of water and debated...run or stay?

Should I get in the con or dive into the well deck? My butt was pretty much unprotected just then, my flak jacket and pot were in the con, and I was wearing only cut-off pants and my flip-flops. What if I dove in the well deck and the second round hit there? What if I dove in the con and it hit there...screw it.

I remember beginning to move at about the same time I heard the second round, it was going over the boat, believe me you just know these things after a while. I do remember thinking about this and having a debate in my mind! I heard it, I heard it go overhead, I was safe and behind where it was going to hit. I don't even remember being scared, they missed me so it was just sort of 'business as usual'.

That would be just about at the top of the sand dune in front of the boat.

"WHAM!"

Okay...you can't really explain what the sound of a 81MM mortar round sounds like when it hits in the soft sand up there and explodes sending a shower of sand into the air. The next one was right behind it; 'Chuck' had made his corrections and was on-target with that one. It exploded far back in the compound and I was sure it was in the new chow-hall. There were some rounds after that as my crew came sprinting back over the dune for the boat, they (the rounds) all went into the same area. The new chow-hall was toast, we were safe.

As my guys jogged down the well deck up to the main deck and behind the con with me...I began frying the chicken, it was time to eat anyway.

Beer and Cokes were passed around, greens were chopped up and other things were found to eat with our main course. As the sun set behind the mountains to the west we were very well fed a little drunk and relaxed, a good end to a day on the rivers in the northern part of South Vietnam, Cua Viet, 3.5 miles below the DMZ where the Cua Viet River and the South China Sea meet.

Even when the chow hall was rebuilt we didn't go anywhere near it.

Art Moore and CBMU 301, The SeaBee's

I was going to just give Art Moore credit for providing some of the photos. However, the longer I thought about it, a little more was in order. Both for Art and all of the guys of CBMU 301.

The men of CBMU 301, Detail Charlie had their hands full in the foreword base at Cua Viet, just like all the other areas in I-Corps.

In a lot of places (in country) they could build something then maintain it in some sort of a normal manner...nothing up there was normal. The 'maintenance' they carried out was rebuilding and rebuilding and...more rebuilding. For them it was an almost daily process while continuing to build more of the port facility.

One enemy was the weather at times of the year. The wind coming in off of the North China Sea could peel the tin roofing right off of our hooches, even with sandbags on them. The combination of the wind, the action from the sea and the river played hell with the moorings, barges and anything near the water.

They had to maintain the generators, antennas, hooches, bunkers and everything else around a concrete ramp the size of a football field. Oh, there was also a small problem with our little buddy 'Chuck'. Since our entire area was 'dialed-in', not only by the big guns and rockets up north, but our buddies out in the bush, the job was unending. Build something today...have it blown away tonight...rebuild it...have it blown away two days later.

Art Moore and CBMU 301, The SeaBee's

With permission of BU2 Art Moore.

Keep working, keep repairing and try to stay alive at the same time!

While I was stationed in Cua Viet we (for one reason or another) probably spent something like 30% of our nights living on the boats. Without the Sea Bee's of Detail Charlie that would have been 100% during 1967-68.

If no one else from the boat group ever said it guys:

Thank you, and Welcome Home Brothers!

APPENDIX 1
C-Rations by Meal and Some Other Stuff

I think we (the Navy) were given the 1944-45 era C-Rations as sort of a joke, maybe because no one in charge of things for us really thought we were going to eat them? Or maybe we just got the stuff no one else wanted, I have no idea. When I saw my first 'Rats' meal then realized that the date on it wasn't a joke I did some wondering while eating, mostly 'is this any good?'

By the time I finished my last tour we had eaten our way up to ones packed in the mid 50's which was good, the 'Ham and Mothers' meal was gone! What I didn't understand (then) was that the Vietnamese would actually trade for them, eat them and, if they weren't nailed down, steal them.

You could actually trade two cans of Ham and Lima Beans for a fresh cleaned dressed chicken at the ramp in Dong Ha! A whole B-1 or B-3 unit could be traded for a fully cooked meal...delivered to the boat.

There were four choices of meat in each group. Because there were several 'vintages' of C-Rations issued to us more than four items may be listed in the groups. In our case (with the older C's) all of the cigarettes were non-filter and, due to age, could be completely smoked in about four normal drags.

APPENDIX 1
C-Rations by Meal and Some Other Stuff

The meals came packed in a case of twelve with four 'John Wayne' or P-38 can openers for the case. The Sterno tabs or 'heat-tabs' came separately, most of us used little balls of C-4 (plastic explosive) to cook with anyway. It got things warmed up a lot faster and didn't go out if there was too much wind.

APPENDIX 2
One Outstanding C-Rats Dinner!

Take one chilled Falstaff beer, pull tab, consume.

Open one can of each:

Beefsteak, spaghetti and meatballs, spiced beef, boned chicken, (2) Pimento cheese spread, crackers, berry jam.

Put all meat items in a pot that will hold them and use C-4 to heat them up. Once they are steaming (stir baby stir!) add the cheese spread, (crumpled) crackers and stir more as the cheese spread melts.

Add the berry jam and about 1/4 bottle of hot sauce, stir this in well. Some salt and pepper if you have any.

Open and consume one more beer as the 'essence' of the meal becomes a culinary masterpiece, also open a can or two of bread.

Well, you waited all day…eat up! Have another beer while you're at it, you've earned it in one way or another.

"Oh…that clean tin pie pan and the metal fork are mine…don't even think about it!"

We actually invented the Egg McMuffin (when we had time).

APPENDIX 2
One Outstanding C-Rats Dinner!

To enjoy this exquisite breakfast time treat you needed the following:

One can of the 'bread' which was round and a little over an inch thick; the can of ham and eggs (about the same thickness), one can of one of the cheese spread(s) and a can of ham slices. It helped to have hot sauce, salt and pepper.

To prepare:

Open the bread and slice it+ in half like a biscuit, open the ham and eggs and cut it in half so it's thinner, get out a slice of the ham. Pop a chunk of C-4 in the stove and brown the underside of the bread over it until golden brown. You have to use C-4 because the sterno tab leaves one bad awful taste behind! Okay, the C-4 doesn't taste too good either, but it was better than the heat tabs, believe me!

Set these aside and do the same with the egg slice and ham slice, set them on the bread. Spread a liberal amount of the cheese spread on top, add salt pepper and hot sauce.

Put the top on and you got breakfast fit for Ronald McDonald!

Toss this delight down with a canteen cup of vintage C's coffee, follow it up with a Chesterfield from about 1947 and you are ready to begin another day on the river!

'HOOOOOOOOO RAAAAAAAAAAAA!'

Other Acknowledgements

My heartfelt thanks to everyone below who assisted in one way or another, contributing a piece of a memory to this book.

Mr. Don and Mrs. Thelma Cain ('Frosty's' parents), for the contribution of several photographs both of him and activities around the Tan My base.

Robert Kilkelly, AKA: Bruce Harvey, for jogging my memory enough to put all of the pieces together about the 860 boat, 'Blueberry Pie' in 'Dodge City'.

'The Colonel' R. M. Johnston, Sr., my late father, "Just write the damned book, it will work out."

My sister Kareen Tucker-Johnston, for saving that one picture of me for all of the years...until I really needed it for something special...thanks sis.

List of websites dealing with the Vietnam War, most are unit sites with pictures and history of a specific unit or area.

The Official Vietnam Veterans website: http://grunt.space.edu

Pretty much the official Brownwater Navy website

http://brownwater-navy.com/vietnam/hawley1.htm

The Home of Task Force 116-The Gamewardens of Vietnam

http://www.tf116.org

Other Acknowledgements

Home of the Swift Boats of the Cua Viet Patrol Area with information of their operations and some very good pictures of the Cua Viet Base.

http://www.pcf45.com

The Amgrunts of 3rd Marines/2nd Amtrac Battalion

http://www.amtrac.org/2atbn

A very nice site built around the Sea Bees that built and repaired/maintained everything in the northern area of I-Corps

http://www.geocities.com/cbmu301/

A very comprehensive site about C-Rations

http://www.homestead.com/gruntfixer

These are only a short list of all possible links. Every one of them has its own list of links inside which could be a book in itself if compiled.

APPENDIX 3
Glossary of Navy/Vietnam Era Slang and Terms

Our war, not unlike any other, had its own vocabulary. We had our own terms and slang for a lot of things. This was added to and enriched by the Vietnamese we associated with. I say enriched because their combination of the Viet language, a little French and pigeon English thrown together, then adding some English letters that they just couldn't get their tongues around, made for some strange words and phrases.

10 Days and a Wake-Up: the amount of time someone had left to do in-country, the 'Wake-Up' was the last day when you caught the 'Big Bird' back to 'The World'.

AmGrunt(s): Marines that normally were mounted on Amtrak's (boxy amphibious track vehicles), up north they also did foot patrol so they were also 'Grunts'.

ARVN: Army of the Republic of Vietnam (the ones on our side)

B-40: military designation for an RPG, 40MM in total diameter at the warhead.

Backing-down: the term for backing up a boat, reverse.

Glossary of Navy/Vietnam Era Slang and Terms

Beatle Nut(s): something like a sunflower seed that older men and women chewed, it blackened the teeth after a while and left a permanent stain on them.

Big-PX also Land of The Big-PX: another term for the USA.

Boats: the abbreviation of the Naval rate Boatswain's mate. The rating is most common aboard ships in the fleet but being boat handlers they drove most of the boats in the Brown Water Navy.

Bom-Ne-Ba: 33 beer, the official beer of Vietnam. Compared to the stuff we got from 'The World' it was like JP-4. It also had no preservatives in it like the stuff that was shipped to us.

Boom-boom: Vietnamese slang for sex or having sex.

Boonies: in the field or forward area.

Boucoup/Boo-Coo: French word used by the Vietnamese all the time 'Big'

Broach: the act of placing a boat parallel to current or surf while making a landing, dangerous condition, could become beached or capsized.

Bunker: any reinforced fighting position (usually sandbags and heavy timber), a place of safety with only a door opening where we hid during any kind of shelling by the bad guys.

Butter-bar: lowest ranking officer with a single golden insignia bar. Not worn in the 'boonies'.

C-4: plastic explosive also a reinforced position just north of the base at Cua Viet. A small ball of it (about the size of a marble) could be used for cooking. It would boil a canteen cup of water in a few minutes.

C-Rats: C-Rations, also called simply C's, the field ration at the time.

Charlie: the most common reference to the Viet Cong or guerillas.

'Cherry': an affectionate term for someone new 'in-country' and hadn't seen any combat action yet.

Chuck: the black term used for a white guy or another common shortened way of referring to the enemy.

Claymore: a directional anti-personnel mine that released hundreds of shrapnel pieces when set off.

Comshaw: the Navy slang for 'borrowing' or misappropriating something that you really need IE: spare parts that are impossible to get through normal channels.

Con: the control area of any boat where the steering, throttles and gauges are located.

Cyclo-girl/boy: prostitute (yes they had both).

Di-di: Vietnamese slang for go away, add Mou to it and it meant go away fast.

Fender: Navy or boating term, fend-off, we used old truck or airplane tires hung over the sides of the boats with rope or cable so that the sides didn't rub together.

G.I.: to them we were all GI's no matter what branch of the service you were in.

Greens: reference to the green uniform of the Marines/Army also our standard uniform in the 'boonies' on ops.

Grunt: ground based Marines. Some of the best guys in the whole world.

Ham-N-Eggs: slang for a fragmentation hand grenade.

Ham and Mothers: the ham and Lima beans C-ration meal that was horrible!

Hanoi-Hanna: the female propaganda radio announcer of North Vietnam. We didn't really pay much attention to the propaganda but she played good rock-n-roll with a little war protest music thrown in.

Hooch or Hootch: where you lived in a normal secure or semi-secure area. 2 X 4/6 and plywood construction, set up off the ground. The top four feet of the walls were screened in; most had a roof covered by a large tent.

Huey: everyone's term when referring to the UH helicopter.

In the Shit: used to describe a battle, firefight etc.

LAW: acronym for a light anti-tank weapon, used as anti-personal weapons and bunker-busters along the rivers. Small and easy to carry but like a bazooka they had back blast so you made sure there was no one behind you when you fired one!

Lazarette: after compartment on an LCM, in our case the steering gear (rudder actuation) was there as well as the fuel tanks. A storage area as well or sleeping area in bad weather.

LCM-8: also referred to as a Mike-8/Eight-boat, at that time, 'the' best shallow draft seaworthy medium landing craft anyone in the world had. One hell of a boat!

Million Dollar Wound: a wound bad enough to get you sent back to 'The World' but not bad enough to cause permanent disability.

Momma-san (son): older Vietnamese woman, wife mother.

MPC: military payment certificate also called 'funny money' or 'Monopoly Money' because the bills looked nothing like real currency.

Nasty Class Boats: the successor to our old PT boat. Very fast and heavily armed the RVN Rangers (on our side but sometimes you wondered) used them to disrupt shipping and smuggling on the South China Sea. Also used to get in and out fast when putting RVN Rangers ashore.

Noc-nam: a very rancid fermented fish sauce used on almost everything.

Numba-one: very good, the best.

Numba-ten: bad or very bad.

Numba-sixty nine: the absolute total worst of anything!

Ops: shortened version of operations or costal operations, anywhere out of the Da Nang area along the coast or up a river.

P-38: slang, the name given to the C-Rations can opener. They were simple worked well and had a hole that allowed you to put a 'keeper' on your dog-tags.

Papa-san (son): older Vietnamese man, father/husband.

PBR: small fast (usually) light river patrol boat.

Pop Flare: a small hand-held self-contained parachute flare.

Pot: your metal helmet, also some of the very good stuff we got to smoke.

Pusher Boat: these were usually a modified LCM-6 they were used as small tugs or pushers to position barges and other boats.

Ramp: the bow or front door of landing craft which can be raised and lowered, also a gently sloping area (constructed) along a river where the craft can be loaded and/or unloaded.

Rats: the common abbreviation for C-rations...also the real rodent that most bunkers were full of.

RPG-B-40: after the war in Iraq everyone knows what these are. The older ones were slower and mostly inaccurate after a few hundred feet but still deadly.

Subic: Subic Bay Naval Base in the Philippines, where most of the boats were sent back to for major overhauls.

Short or Short-Timer: someone nearing the end of his tour was 'getting short', not many days left in-country.

Snipe: Naval nickname given to any fireman (as in boilerman), engineer, mechanic or engine repairman.

Sorry Bou Dat G.I.: general apology or concern for something bad (usually said but never meant) we tossed it around for everything after a while. Beat a guy good at cards and you said that as you raked in the cash or rather the 'funny-money'.

Spider Hole: a small dug-out just large enough to hide a man in, they would then attack out of them.

Splibs: slang term for a black guy.

Spooks: slang term in reference to CIA field officers. We hauled our share of them up and down the rivers.

Striker: a non-rated sailor (usually seaman in rate) that is studying for a trade and advancement. As in 'He's a snipe striker.'

Strip-Clip: a small metal 'clip' which held only the rear of a group of rifle rounds. It clipped over a receiver on the rear top of a rifle magazine allowing for fast reloading of the magazine.

Tee-Tee: Vietnamese/French slang meaning 'very small'.

Trip Flare: a medium sized flare that could be rigged with a trip wire on or around a perimeter; someone 'tripping' the wire would set off (launch) the flare and give away movement by illuminating the area.

U-Boat: LCU/YFU, larger (than a Mike-8) landing craft but, except for the Skylak class much slower. What we couldn't do in loads we made up for in multiple trips to their one.

Willie-Peter: slang term for a white phosphorus round of any kind.

World or 'The World': referring to almost anywhere but Vietnam, most commonly used in talking about the USA.

There are probably some terms that I missed but hey, Sorry bou Dat G.I.!

The author in 2015 on a boat ride in Hoi An.

"The 'bad guys' always fired first."

Hauling one more load of cargo in a 'Duck Pond', the Cua Viet River (or any other river) in the I-Corps area of South Vietnam. The load in their well deck is essential to the survival of both the Marines and Army troops stationed a convoy away from disaster. Twelve miles of unsecured river (from the base at Cua Viet to Dong Ha) during every trip 'driving' past the shattered, half-sunken hulks in the river that didn't make it. Just like targets…in a shooting gallery…

Thirty-seven years after his war ended, a Vietnam 'River-Rat' finally tells part of the story of a small Navy river unit that has gone undocumented and all but forgotten, the medium LCM-8 cargo boats of Costal Operations, NSA Da Nang.

During three tours of duty 'driving' a medium landing craft while hauling every kind of cargo on every river in the I-Corps of South Vietnam, Bob Johnston reaches back for memories. Beginning in Da Nang in 1965 and ending in the summer of 1968 in Cua Viet, he shares stories that range from laughable to sad to plain horrific. Sometimes the things that happened on the rivers could be compared to 'M.A.S.H.' while other events were moments of intense white-hot bone rattling fear that he has never forgotten.

Brief intense firefights with an unseen enemy on the riverbanks, the units devotion to duty and hard work that earned them two 'Naval

Unit Commendations' for 'Outstanding Performance under the Most Adverse Conditions' then a 'Presidential Unit Citation' during the Tet Offensive in 1968 for keeping the vital Cua Viet river supply lines open...no matter what.

Leading the crew of 'Blueberry Pie', the lone ferry linking two sections of Highway 1 in 'Arizona Territory', twenty miles south of Da Nang. One boat, two companies of beleaguered US Marines...surrounded by almost 1800 well motivated NVA troops.

Taking cover in a sandbag bunker during an almost nightly artillery or rocket attack while living and working just under four miles south of the DMZ. The unflinching heroism of his (often green) crewmen, the admiration for the Marines that they re-supplied and who protected them, sometimes with great loss of life.

He also speaks of the mind and soul, the mind-numbing hopelessness that takes you over when you spend so many days just trying to 'do it' one more time while trying to forget that you may not see another day. Backing over a hundred tons of loaded boat off the ramp at Cua Viet one more time...his crew checking the weapons...getting into flak jackets and pots while going to full throttle...a lone boat on a shallow brown river making what should be the last trip of the day, the entire crew up and 'on point'. Always wondering...would 'Charlie' make this the last trip of their lives?

APPENDIX 3
Glossary of Navy/Vietnam Era Slang and Terms

The End

Made in the USA
Lexington, KY
30 October 2017